NEW, REVISED
EDITION

# COLOR
# DESIGN
# WORKBOOK

Quarto is the authority on a wide range of topics.

Quarto educates, entertains and enriches the lives of
our readers—enthusiasts and lovers of hands-on living.

www.QuartoKnows.com

© 2008, 2017 Quarto Publishing Group USA Inc.
Revised edition published in 2017

This edition published in 2017 by Rockport Publishers, an imprint
of The Quarto Group,
100 Cummings Center, Suite 265-D, Beverly, MA 01915, USA.
T (978) 282-9590 F (978) 283-2742 QuartoKnows.com

Rockport Publishers titles are also available at discount for retail,
wholesale, promotional, and bulk purchase. For details, contact
the Special Sales Manager by email at specialsales@quarto.com
or by mail at The Quarto Group, Attn: Special Sales Manager, 401
Second Avenue North, Suite 310, Minneapolis, MN 55401, USA.

**Originally found under the following Library of Congress
Cataloging-in-Publication Data**
Adams, Sean.
    Color design workbook : a real-world guide to using color
in graphic design / by Sean Adams, with Terry Stone
designed by Sean Adams ;
        p.     cm.
    ISBN 1-59253-192-X (hardcover)
    1.Graphic Arts—Technique. 2. Commercial art—Themes,
motives. 3. Color in advertising. 4. Color in design.
5. Color—Psychological aspects. I. Adams, Sean.
II. Title.
NC1000.S76 2006
741.6—dc22                              2005014277

ISBN-13: 978-1-63159-292-8

10 9 8 7 6 5 4 3 2 1

The color swatches contained in this book are as accurate as
possible. However, due to the nature of the four-color printing
proccess, slight variations can occur due to ink balancing
on press. Every effort has been made to minimize these
variations.

# NEW, REVISED EDITION

# COLOR DESIGN WORKBOOK

## A REAL-WORLD GUIDE TO USING COLOR IN GRAPHIC DESIGN

**SEAN ADAMS**
WITH TERRY LEE STONE

ROCKPORT

# Contents

# "I'm afraid of color."

This is a comment made too often by designers. There is a perception that a discrete and complex set of rules applies to color, and one wrong choice will lead to failure. There are, indeed, rules that apply to color theory. These are based on laws of physics, wavelengths of light, and how our eyes perceive the world. We know from experience that a specific shade of red and blue will create an optical vibration. We understand that high contrast is easier to see than subtle tones. And we realize that each color has cultural, emotional, and personal meanings.

This fear leads to the action of selecting only the "safe" colors. The tried and true colors in a default digital palette must be correct. The result is work that feels expected and ordinary. Extraordinary work is the result of unique colors applied with confidence and clarity. There is a reason why a Van Gogh demands our attention while a paint by numbers composition may be pleasant, but flat. As Tibor Kalman said, "If you only do work no one will hate, no one will love it." This statement could not be more true when working with color.

The secret is that the only way to apply color incorrectly is to do so hesitantly. Any color palette will work if it is employed with courage and knowledge. The designer, must also have the ability to explain why one palette is better than the other. He or she must persuade the client why the warm shade of red is "on brand" while purple isn't.

The designer today is faced with multiple media and delivery options. The ability to control every reproduction of a corporate color is antiquated. But a proprietary palette and clear color choice will outperform the mild mannered and expected every time. —*Sean Adams*

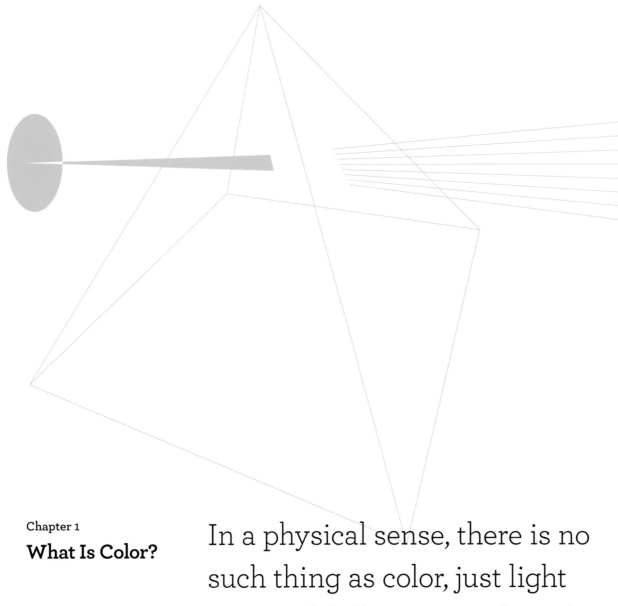

Chapter 1
**What Is Color?**

In a physical sense, there is no such thing as color, just light waves of different wavelengths.

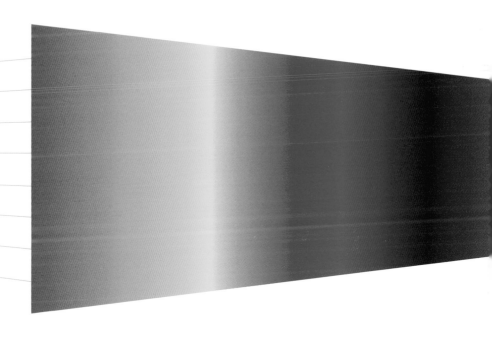

The human eye can distinguish among these wavelengths, so we see the world in color. Rays of light vibrate at different speeds. The sensation of color, which happens in our brains, is a result of our vision's response to these different wavelengths. When taken together, the various rays our eyes can distinguish are called the visible spectrum. This fairly narrow range of colors includes red, orange, yellow, green, blue, blue-violet (which scientists call indigo), and violet.

**The visible spectrum.**
The colors that the human eye can experience are expressed in this gradient graphic. Reds have the longest wavelengths, violets the shortest. Contained in a ray of light but invisible to the human eye are infrared colors (below red in the visible spectrum) and ultraviolet (above violet in the visible spectrum). In addition in the visible spectrum, the eye perceives black and white. White contains all colors of the spectrum and is sometimes described as an achromatic color. Black is the absence of all color—no visible light reaches the eye. Alternatively, an exhaustive combination of multiple pigments can reflect so little light that the eye perceives black.

## Apparent Color

Color is derived from light, either natural or artificial. With little light, little or no color is present. With a lot of light comes lots of color. Strong light produces intense color.

### Seeing in Color

Our eyes have three types of color receptor cells, or cones: red, green, and blue. As a result, all incoming light is reduced to these three colors. All perceived colors are generated by a mixture of these three colors. However, not every color can be seen by humans; those that can are therefore called the *visible spectrum*. People can distinguish approximately 10 million colors; this visible spectrum is called the *human color space*. Not everyone's color-sensing cells respond alike, so identification of a specific color is highly subjective.

The study of color is where art and science meet, with numerous theories from both disciplines coming into play. It can thus be difficult to comprehend. To understand color perception, we need to understand the physics of light, which causes and affects our ideas of primary colors.

### Primary Colors

There are two types of primary color: additive and subtractive. As noted, our eyes have red, green, and blue (RGB) color receptors. RGB are the primary colors of pure light and are referred to as *additive* primary colors. The *subtractive* primary colors, made from reflected light, fall into two types: the printer's primaries, which are cyan, magenta, and yellow (CMY), and the artist's primaries, which are red, yellow, and blue (RYB). Artists' primaries, though nonscientific, are used as the basis for most color theory (*see chapter two*).

Designers utilize all three types of primary colors. They select colors using RYB and color theories. Then they generate layouts on computer screens in RGB, and then perhaps translate them into ink on paper with CMY—plus K, or black—to form the CMYK of four-color process lithography.

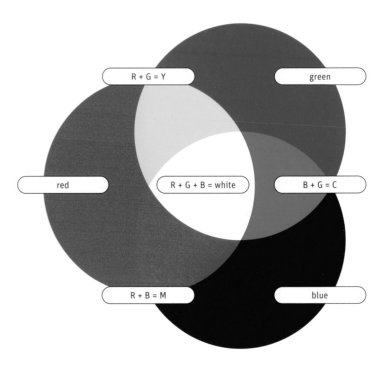

**Additive Mixing (RGB Model)**

R + G = Y

green

red

R + G + B = white

B + G = C

R + B = M

blue

**Additive Color: The RGB Primaries (Light)**

Visible spectrum colors are pure and represent the greatest possible brightness or intensity. Designers working with rays of colored light, as on computer screens, use additive colors, or RGB. When these colors overlap, other colors are produced: red and blue light form cyan; red and green light form yellow; and green and blue light form magenta. When all three additive primaries overlap, white light is produced. Thus, white light is the combined presence of all color wavelengths. We call them additive because all together, these primaries create white. RGB reflects actual human color receptors. Mixtures of these primary colors produce a large part of the human color experience. Television sets, computer monitors, cameras, and color scanners all produce mixtures of red, green, and blue light.

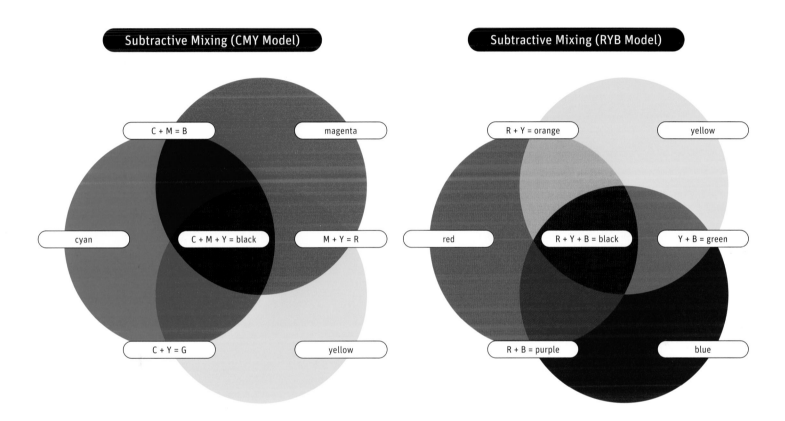

### Subtractive Mixing (CMY Model)

- C + M = B
- magenta
- cyan
- C + M + Y = black
- M + Y = R
- C + Y = G
- yellow

### Subtractive Mixing (RYB Model)

- R + Y = orange
- yellow
- red
- R + Y + B = black
- Y + B = green
- R + B = purple
- blue

### Subtractive Color: The CMY Primaries (Transparent Pigments)

All objects have physical properties that cause them to absorb some color waves and reflect others. Color, when applied to a surface such as canvas or paper, has the same characteristic. The sensation of color is produced when a surface absorbs all the wavelengths except those the eyes perceive. When color is experienced through reflected light, it is called *subtractive*. There are two sets of subtractive primary colors: the artist's primaries—red, yellow, and blue (RYB)—and the printer's primaries—cyan, magenta, and yellow (CMY) transparent inks and dyes. Coupled with black, known as K, we get CMYK, or four-color process. Each of these triads is combined to produce all visible color. In the subtractive CMY model, magenta combines with yellow to form red, yellow and cyan form green, and cyan and magenta form violet (purple). In the case of both versions of the subtractive primaries, when all the primary colors are combined, black is produced—that is, no color is reflected.

### Subtractive Color: The RYB Primaries (Opaque Pigments)

In the RYB triad, red combines with yellow to produce orange, red and blue create violet (purple), and blue and yellow create green. RYB, the primary color system used in art classes, forms the basis of most color theory. As with CMY, when all the primary colors are combined, black is produced—no color is reflected. The secondary colors produced by the three triads indicate the purity of the colors that can be obtained by the different mixing methods. RGB produces pure CMY as secondary colors, and the CMY triad produces RGB as secondary colors, but they are duller than pure RGB light. The secondary colors resulting from RYB are even duller than those in the RGB or CMY triads.

## The Properties of Color

Whether using the additive or subtractive primaries, each color must be described in terms of its physical properties. These properties are independent of each other, and each one must be measured or defined in order to fully describe the color. Scientific descriptions of color, or *colorimetry*, involve the specification of these color properties in either a subjective or objective system of measurement. The subjective system describes color in terms of hue, saturation, and brightness (HSB), while the objective system measures the dominant wavelength, purity, and luminance of colors.

*Hue* is the common name of a color that indicates its position in the visible spectrum or on the color wheel. Hue is determined by the specific wavelength of the color in a ray of light. The description of a hue can be made more precise in comparison to the next hue (e.g., a certain blue might be more accurately called blue-green). *Saturation* refers to the intensity, strength, purity, or chroma—the absence of black, white, or gray—in a color. A vivid color has high or full saturation, whereas a dull one is de-saturated. Saturation is a measure of the richness of a color. *Brightness*, or value, is the relative degree of lightness or darkness of a color, or its reflective quality or brilliance. A color can be more narrowly described as either light or dark (e.g., light blue or dark blue). The brightness of a color is changed by mixing it with white (to form a *tint*) or with black (to form a *shade*) in varying proportions. Graphic design software programs have tools for varying the HSB of colors.

Objective color notation was developed by the Commission Internationale de l'Eclairage (CIE) to provide a mathematical model for describing color. The CIE (in English, the International Commission on Illumination) is an international technical, scientific, and cultural nonprofit organization that sets standards on the science and art of lighting, vision, and colorimetry. Though CIE notation is not used by designers, it underpins color management in modern digital devices.

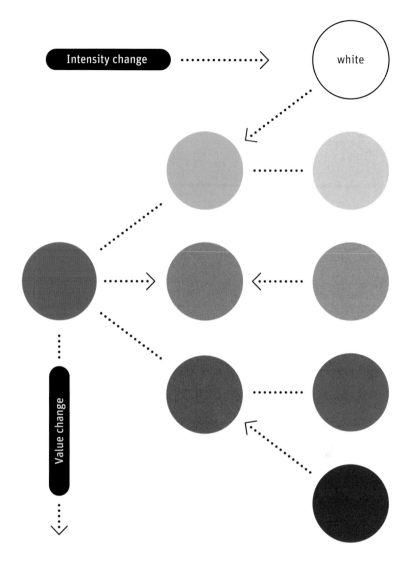

This chart demonstrates changes in saturation and value by adding or subtracting black, white, or gray. When white is added to a bright red, the value is lighter, and the resulting color is less saturated. Adding black to the red results in a dark red closer to the neutral scale because of saturation changes. If gray is added, the saturation is lowered, but the value is unchanged.

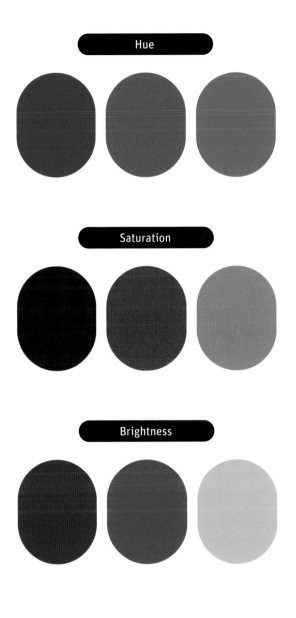

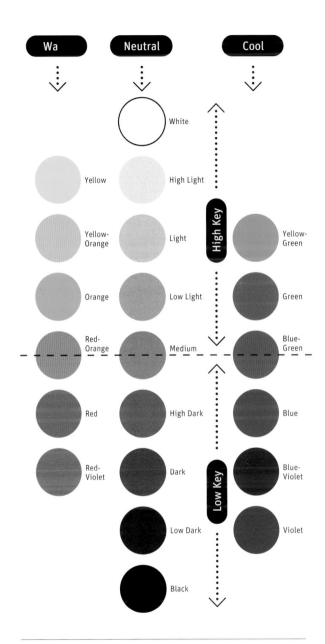

This chart demonstrates HSB. The top row shows three blue hues, the middle row is an example of three degrees of saturation of a particular blue, and the bottom row demonstrates three levels of brightness, or values, of blue.

This chart shows relative values of hues at their maximum saturation. The dotted rule indicates the midpoint. All colors above the line are high key, while those below the line are low key. Warm, cool, and neutral relationships are also indicated.

**Chapter 2**

# Color Theory

### What Is Color Theory?

Color theory is a set of parameters that provide guidance to mixing color. It is the principle of primary colors, red, blue, and yellow mixing to create all other colors. Color theory addresses issues of value and tone, darkness and lightness. And it is applied to how we see color on the visible spectrum. Diagrams, such as color wheels and triangles, help designers understand the theories and color interactions. A well-produced chart can be the tool to select and combine colors to construct harmony and power.

Diagrams such as this color wheel, which shows pure hues as well as tints and shades, serve as a guide for selecting and combining colors beyond the pure hues. Different color theory diagrams have different purposes. Some are simple and some are complex, but all are useful references when thinking about color and choosing color palettes.

# A Brief History of Color Theory

Many measurement systems, but all color theory has one goal: to explain color relationships with an aim to create harmony.

We offer this brief account to familiarize designers with the major color theorists and their significant findings. We encourage further exploration of this topic to gain a deeper understanding of color theory.

Since ancient times, color theorists have developed ideas and interpretations of color relationships. Attempts to formalize and recognize order date back at least to Aristotle (384–322 B.C.E.) but began in earnest with Leonardo da Vinci (1452–1519) and have progressed ever since. Leonardo noted that certain colors intensify each other, discovering *contrary* or *complementary* colors. The first color wheel was invented by Britain's Sir Isaac Newton (1642–1727), who split white light into red, orange, yellow, green, blue, indigo, and violet beams, then joined the two ends of the spectrum to form a circle showing the natural progression of colors. When Newton created the color wheel, he noticed that mixing two colors from opposite positions produced a neutral or *anonymous* color.

More than a century later, while studying the psychological effects of color, Germany's famed poet and playwright Johann Wolfgang von Goethe (1749–1832) furthered color theory. Goethe divided all colors into two groups. On the plus side he put the warm colors (red to orange to yellow) and on the minus side the cool colors (green to blue to violet). He noted that colors on the plus side produced excitement in viewers, while he associated the minus-side colors with unsettled feelings. In 1810 Goethe published *Zur Farbenlehre* (*Theory of Color*), in which he disagreed

with Newton's conclusions about color. He believed that a scientific approach alone did not enable one to fully understand color. Goethe's observations of the human perception of color, rather than just the physics of light, allowed him to discover important aspects of color theory, including simultaneous contrast and color's relationship to emotion.

Louis Prang (1824–1909) was an influential pioneer of American chromolithographs and a noted educator whose 1876 book *Theory of Color* helped popularize the theory of red, yellow, and blue primary colors in American art education. Wilhelm Ostwald (1853–1932), a Russian-German Nobel Prize–winning chemist, developed a color system related to psychological harmony and order in the 1916 *Die Farbenfibel* (*The Color Primer*). His ideas about color harmony influenced future color theorists and the Dutch de Stijl art movement (see page 100).

The next major set of theories comes from the Bauhaus, the highly influential German art and design school (1919–1933) that focused on the integration of art and industry, encouraging an ideology of functional design. Bauhaus member Johannes Itten (1888–1967) was a Swiss color and art theorist who developed *color chords* and modified the color wheel. Itten's color wheel is based on a primary triad of red, yellow, and blue, and includes twelve hues. He studied color in terms of both design and science, and his experiments with light waves explored color relationships and visual effects. Following Goethe's lead, Itten delved into the psychological and spiritual aspects of color. His most important work, *The Art of*

*Color,* is summarized in his treatise called *Itten: The Elements of Color.* Itten's theories still form the core of most art school color information.

Josef Albers (1888–1976) studied under Itten and also taught at the Bauhaus. His abstract art used mathematical proportions to achieve balance and unity. After immigration to the United States, his teachings at Yale University led to his book *Interaction of Color,* a crucial text on color theory. Albers' focus is on what happens when colors interact, and his experiments are a resource for creating subtle color compositions. Faber Birren (1900–1988) explored the relationship between color and expression. His research helped clarify the historical development of the triadic color system.

The American artist Albert Munsell (1858–1918) created a new and versatile color model around 1905. Munsell was inspired by the work of fellow American Nicholas Ogden Rood (1831–1902) and German painter Philip Otto Runge (1777–1810) to develop a three-dimensional color model that demonstrates relationships between full-spectrum hues as well as tints and shades. Munsell's important realization was that, when pure, some hues are more saturated than others, so color relationships are distorted when forced into a circle. He created what is known as the Munsell Tree, with hues arranged along branches of different lengths in order of saturation. Munsell's work was adopted by American industry as its material standard for naming colors. It has also influenced the color-space modeling of the CIE (Commission International de l'Eclairge).

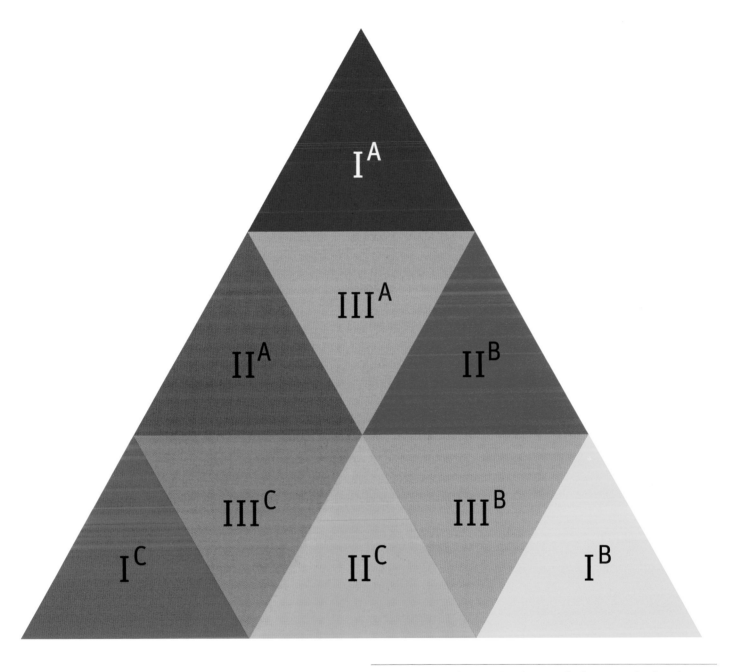

The Goethe color triangle is an equilateral triangle subdivided into nine equilateral triangles. The three primary colors (blue is I^A, and so on) are arranged on the outer edges, with secondary (purple is II^A, and so on) and tertiary (lavender is III^A, and so on) colors located inside. This is one method Goethe used to demonstrate color relationships. He believed that colors are linked to emotion, and his diagram demonstrates these connections. For example, he called I^C, II^C, III^C, and II^A a serene color scheme. Here again, the designation is completely subjective, as is true in nearly all color theories.

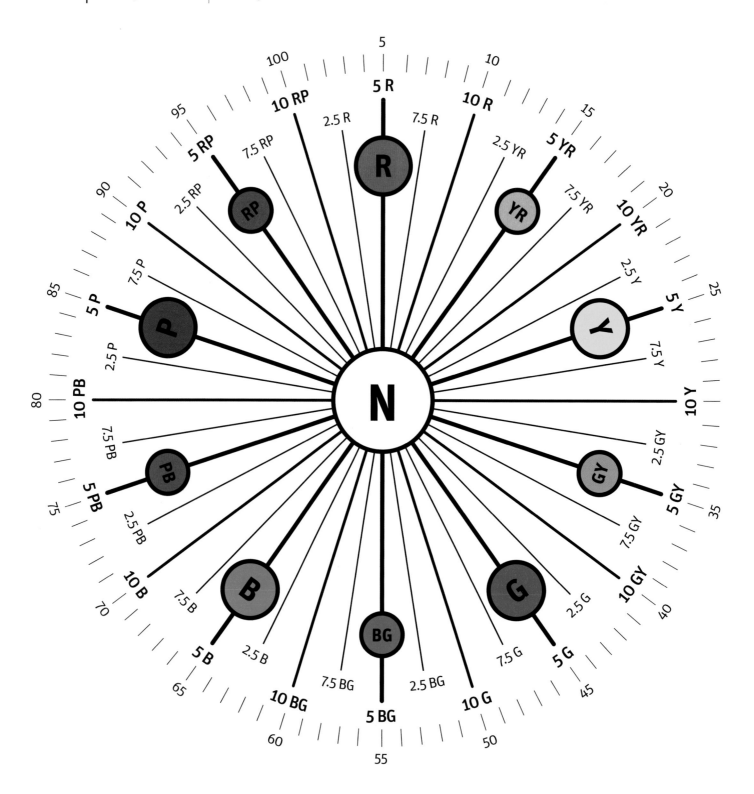

**Left**

The Munsell Color Tree, when shown as a wheel (left), is divided into five primary or principal hues (R stands for red, y for yellow, etc.). Five intermediaries are also labeled with the initials of the surrounding principals (YR for yellow-red, etc.), producing a total of ten divisions. For even more accurate specification, the circle is divided into steps numbered clockwise from 5, at the top, to 100.

This diagram is useful because it explains the rationale behind the Munsell color notation system. Designers may need to use the Munsell color notation system when specifying colors in manufacturing processes such as packaging and environmental design projects.

**Right**

Johannes Itten held that color harmony was subjective. However, he developed a series of diagrams, such as these, for the construction of harmonious triads (three-color combinations, top) and tetrads (four-color combinations, below) in twelve-part color wheels. These groups of hues relate in pleasing ways. Spinning the center triangles or rectangles provides other successful combinations.

**Above**

His twelve-pointed star expands on the idea of a color wheel by showing hues along with tints and shades. The color star is a more complex diagram of color interactions.

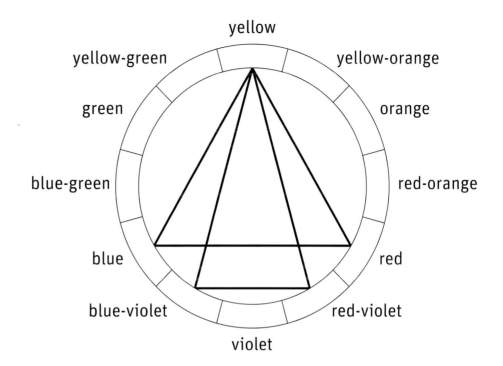

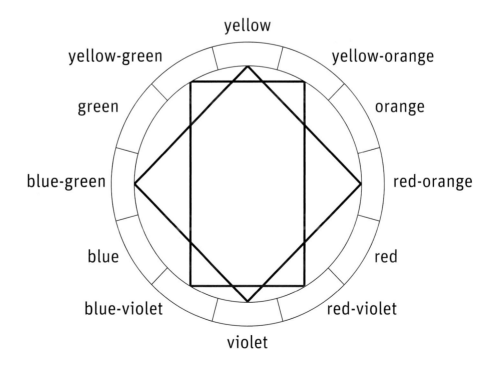

**Color theory is, at its core, about developing aesthetically pleasing color relationships.**

One of the best tools for visualizing color relationships is the color wheel. This wheel, originally developed by Sir Isaac Newton, can be constructed with just a few colors, or can be quite complex incorporating many color variations. Perhaps the most useful version is the twelve-step color wheel containing twelve equidistant pure hues, as shown below.

Successful color relationships can be referred to as "color harmonies." Whether they consist of similar hues that are soothing to the eye or are made of contrasting ones that excite the eye, color harmonies are often subject to personal preference. However, the study of art and design has given us some specific color theories, or guiding principles, that help us make effective decisions about color usage.

We recommend the use of the color wheel called the Subtractive Artists' Primary Colors (RYB), because picking colors is easiest with this set of primaries. The color wheel will help to select color combinations that balance each other. This balance is a result of all the colors in a chosen composition adding up to gray, or neutrality, in the eye/brain. This result will cause the work to just "feel right" to the viewer.

A color by itself will elicit an emotional and physical response, but the nature of the response can be altered by placing it in context with one or more colors. Color perceptions shift dynamically when aligned with other colors. Designers can vary color combinations to produce relationships that are allied or contrasting and therefore can affect viewers' impression.

**12 Step Color Wheel**

red · red orange · orange · orange yellow · yellow · yellow green · green · green blue · blue · blue purple · purple · purple red

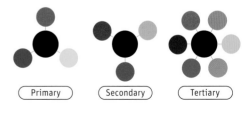

Primary    Secondary    Tertiary

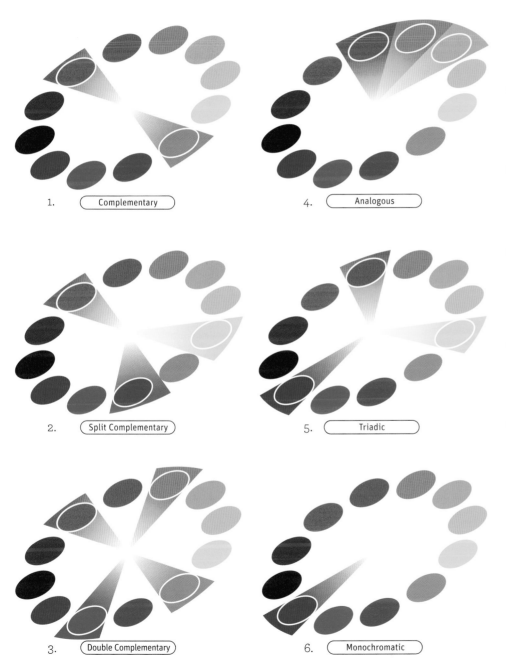

1.          Complementary

4.          Analogous

2.          Split Complementary

5.          Triadic

3.          Double Complementary

6.          Monochromatic

## Color Harmony

Here are six basic color relationship concepts that can be applied to an infinite number of color combinations.

**1. Complementary**

These are color pairs that are directly opposite each other on the color wheel. They represent the most contrasting relationships. The use of two complementary colors will cause a visual vibration and excite the eye.

**2. Split Complementary**

These are the three-color schemes in which one color is accompanied by two others that are spaced equally from the first color's complement. The contrast is toned down somewhat, providing a more sophisticated relationship.

**3. Double Complementary**

This is the combination of two pairs of complementary colors. As complements increase the apparent intensity of each other, not all color sets will be pleasing. Avoid using equal volumes of the four colors to make the scheme less jarring.

**4. Analogous**

These are combinations of two or more colors that are spaced equally from each other on the color wheel. These colors have similar light ray wavelengths, so they are easiest on the eye.

**5. Triadic**

These are combinations of any three colors that are spaced evenly around the color wheel. Triads with primaries are garish, but secondary and tertiary triads provide softer contrast. Triads in which two of the colors share a common primary (e.g., purple and orange share red) may seem more pleasing.

**6. Monochromatic**

These are color schemes made up of shades and tints of a single color. Use one hue and explore variety in saturation and lightness to form an allied combination of similar colors.

Rejecting the classic tradition of one or two color logos, Carbone Smolan designed an identity for Shuttersong with a bright and varied palette. Shuttersong® is an application that allows the user to effortlessly combine digital images with sound and share them everywhere. The multicolored mermaid reinforces this friendly and colorful mission.
**Carbone Smolan**

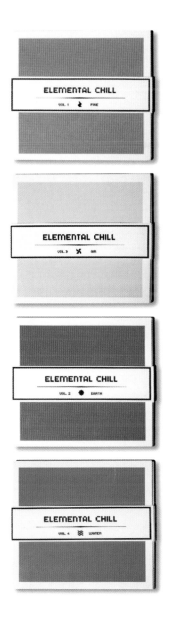

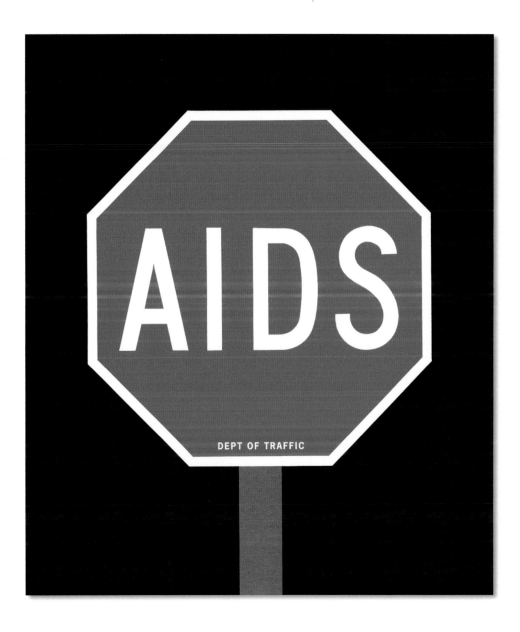

The packaging of the music CD series *Elemental Chill* has a beautiful palette of sophisticated muted colors in orange, red, green, and blue. When selecting a color scheme, it is important to consider the use of tints and shades of hues in order to create a pleasing and harmonious balance in the color system. Referring to color theory diagrams such as Itten's color star, shown on page 15, allows designers to visualize color interactions.
**Karlsson Wiliker**

This poster addresses the immediacy and gravity of the AIDS epidemic. Black, red, and white, three of the colors with the highest contrast, are deftly used with confidence and simplicity. The bright red stop sign shape acts as a clear and aggressive target and reinforce the message. Only white typography is used to simplify the composition .
**Steff Geissbühler**

**Chapter 3**

# Color Meanings

The human eye and brain experience color physically, mentally, and emotionally. As a result, colors themselves have meanings. Color symbolism is often a cultural agreement, and opinions about the associations are varied and sometimes conflicting. The Color Index charts on the following pages provide a sampling of color meanings, associations, and anecdotal information about color. Be sure to investigate a particular color's meanings and associations before using it in a design project.

# Color Index

Primary

| | Color | Associated with | Positive | Negative |
|---|---|---|---|---|
| | Red | fire<br>blood<br>sex | passion<br>love<br>blood<br>energy<br>enthusiasm<br>excitement<br>heat<br>power | aggression<br>anger<br>battle<br>revolution<br>cruelty<br>immorality |
| | Yellow | sunshine | intellect<br>wisdom<br>optimism<br>radiance<br>joy<br>idealism | jealousy<br>cowardice<br>deceit<br>caution |
| | Blue | sea<br>sky | knowledge<br>coolness<br>peace<br>masculinity<br>contemplation<br>loyalty<br>justice<br>intelligence | depression<br>coldness<br>detachment<br>apathy |

| Cultural links | In addition | Sample |
|---|---|---|

**Ivory Coast, Africa**
Dark red indicates death.
**France**
Masculinity
**Most of Asia**
Marriage, prosperity, happiness
**India**
Soldier's symbol
**South Africa**
Color of mourning

- Most visually dominant color
- Suggests speed, action
- Stimulates heart rate, breathing, and appetite
- People appear heavier in red clothes.
- Red cars are stolen most often.

For Pastis , the firm, Mucca replicated the feel of an early 20-century French brasserie, introducing a joie de vivre to the industrial Meatpacking District in New York City. Several shades of red are used to convey a classic Parisian flavor that has evolved over time.
**Mucca**

**Buddhist cultures**
Priests wear saffron yellow robes.
**Egypt and Burma**
Signifies mourning
**India**
Symbol of merchant or farmer
**Hindu cultures**
Worn to celebrate the festival of spring
**Japan**
Associated with courage

- First color that the human eye notices
- Brighter than white
- Speeds the metabolism
- Bright yellow is the most fatiguing color; can irritate the eyes.
- Pale yellow can enhance concentration (used for legal pads).

The cover of the *American Photography 17* book shouts to the passersby—the goal of the designer. *AP17* is a handsome 432-page volume that presents the best photography of the year, as selected by a jury of publishing professionals.
**344 Design**

**Most of the world**
Considered a masculine color
**China**
Color for little girls
**Iran**
Color of mourning
**Western bridal tradition**
Means love
**Worldwide**
Most popular corporate color

- Blue food is rare in nature; unappetizing, suppresses hunger.
- Causes the body to produce calming chemicals; relaxing
- People are said to be more productive in blue rooms.
- Blue clothing often symbolizes loyalty or trust.

Doyle Partners designed the slipcase and books for *The Lincoln Anthology*. As part of *The Lincoln Bicentennial Collection* for the Library of America, blue takes prominence, communicating honor, honesty, loyalty, and American patriotism. Red and white are also patriotic colors,
**Doyle Partners**

# Color Index

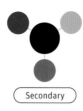

Secondary

| | Color | Associated with | Positive | Negative |
|---|---|---|---|---|
|  | Green | plants<br>the natural<br>environment | fertility<br>money<br>growth<br>healing<br>success<br>nature<br>harmony<br>honesty<br>youth | greed<br>envy<br>nausea<br>poison<br>corrosion<br>inexperience |
| | Purple | royalty<br>spirituality | luxury<br>wisdom<br>imagination<br>sophistication<br>rank<br>inspiration<br>wealth<br>nobility<br>mysticism | exaggeration<br>excess<br>madness<br>cruelty |
| | Orange | autumn<br>citrus | creativity<br>invigoration<br>uniqueness<br>energy<br>vibrancy<br>stimulation<br>sociability<br>health<br>whimsy<br>activity | crassness<br>trendiness<br>loudness |

| Cultural links | In addition | Sample |
|---|---|---|
| **Islam**<br>Green is associated with paradise.<br>**Ireland**<br>Green is strongly associated with Ireland.<br>**Celtic cultures**<br>The Green Man was the god of fertility.<br>**Native American cultures**<br>Green is linked with the will of man. | • Green is the easiest color on the eyes.<br>• Green is a calming and refreshing color, often used in hospitals to relax patients.<br>• Green means "go"; everything is in order.<br>• Green is said to aid digestion and reduce stomachaches. | The U.S. Environmental Protection Agency (EPA) is dedicated to protecting human health and the environment. The obvious choice for the identity was a bright grass green to signify nature.<br>**Chermayeff & Geismar** |
| **Latin America**<br>Purple indicates death.<br>**Thailand**<br>Purple is worn by widows mourning a husband's death.<br>**Japan**<br>Purple represents ceremony, enlightenment, and arrogance. | • Purple has a feminine and romantic quality that is sometimes associated with male homosexuality.<br>• Rare in nature, purple seems artificial.<br>• In ancient times, purple dyes were expensive and worn by royalty and the wealthy only.<br>• Purple is said to enhance the imagination and thus is used in decorating children's rooms. | The poster for the independent film group, Filmforum, satisfies the need for economic printing. The two color printing uses the properties of purple to create drama. The black and white image is low quality. Overprinting purple hides the image's flaws creating a rich texture.<br>**Sean Adams** |
| **Northern Ireland**<br>Orange signifies the Protestant movement.<br>**Native American cultures**<br>Orange is linked with learning and kinship.<br>**India**<br>Orange signifies Hinduism.<br>**Netherlands**<br>Orange is the national color as the Dutch monarchs came from Orange-Nassau. | • Orange is an appetite stimulant.<br>• Orange rooms get people thinking and talking.<br>• Orange rooms speak of friendliness and fun.<br>• Orange is used for visibility enhancement, which is why hunters and highway workers wear it. | The Nickelodeon identity was originally designed by Tom Corey and utilizes white balloon type knocked out of an orange shape. Orange was chosen because it was rarely used in children's products at that time and is a bit irreverent, which captured Nick's point of view. This version of the logo, updated at AdamsMorioka, enhanced the irreverent orange.<br>**AdamsMorioka** |

# Color Index

Neutral

| | Color | Associated with | Positive | Negative |
|---|---|---|---|---|
| | Black | night<br>death | power<br>authority<br>weight<br>sophistication<br>elegance<br>formality<br>seriousness<br>dignity<br>solitude<br>mystery<br>stylishness | fear<br>negativity<br>evil<br>secrecy<br>submission<br>mourning<br>heaviness<br>remorse<br>emptiness |
| | White | light<br>purity | perfection<br>wedding<br>cleanliness<br>virtue<br>innocence<br>lightness<br>softness<br>sacredness<br>simplicity<br>truth | fragility<br>isolation |
| | Gray | neutrality | balance<br>security<br>reliability<br>modesty<br>classicism<br>maturity<br>intelligence<br>wisdom | lack of commitment<br>uncertainty<br>moodiness<br>cloudiness<br>old age<br>boredom<br>indecision<br>bad weather<br>sadness |

| Cultural links | In addition | Sample |
|---|---|---|

**China**
Black is for little boys.
**Asia generally**
Black is associated with career, knowledge, mourning and penance.
**American, European, Japanese youth**
Black is the color of rebellion.
**Worldwide**
Black denotes dark-skinned people of sub-Saharan African ancestry.

- Black clothing makes people look thinner.
- Black humor is morbid.
- Black makes other colors look brighter.
- In color therapy, black is supposed to boost self-confidence and strength.
- Black is often associated with secret societies.

Gordon Parks was an American photographer and filmmaker who documented issues of civil rights, poverty, and the African-American experience. A simple black band and no additional colors allows the dignity of the black and white image of Muhammad Ali to be the prominent communication.
**Sean Adams**

---

**Japan and China**
White is a funeral color.
**Worldwide**
A white flag is a universal symbol for truce.
**North America, Europe**
White denotes light-skinned people of Caucasian ancestry.
**India**
Married women wearing white invite unhappiness.

- In some culture, it's considered good luck to be married in a white garment.
- White is the perfectly balanced color.
- White is so brilliant that it gives some people headaches.
- White light can be blinding.
- White is associated with angels and gods.

Minimal use of graphic elements, primarily the design firm's logo, against a stark white background creates a feeling of open space. The design is an effective self-promotion that celebrates the new year in this 2002 poster.
**344 Design**

---

**Native American**
Gray is associated with honor and friendship.
**Asian**
Gray means helpful people as well as travel.
**America**
The color gray is used to represent industry, in contrast to environmentalism, which is represented by green.
**Worldwide**
Gray is often associated with silver and money.

- Gray seldom evokes strong emotions.
- Gray is a balance of black and white.
- Gray is its own complement.
- Grayscale means rendering an image in a range of blacks and whites. It also refers to a tonal scale of blacks and whites that is used in calibration and accurate reproduction of halftone images.

This promo for fashion designer Anni Kuan features New York Laundromats. The gray effect is achieved by printing black ink on newsprint. The overall effect of the piece is a balanced yet gritty portrait of the city rendered in monochromatic images.
**Sagmeister, Inc**

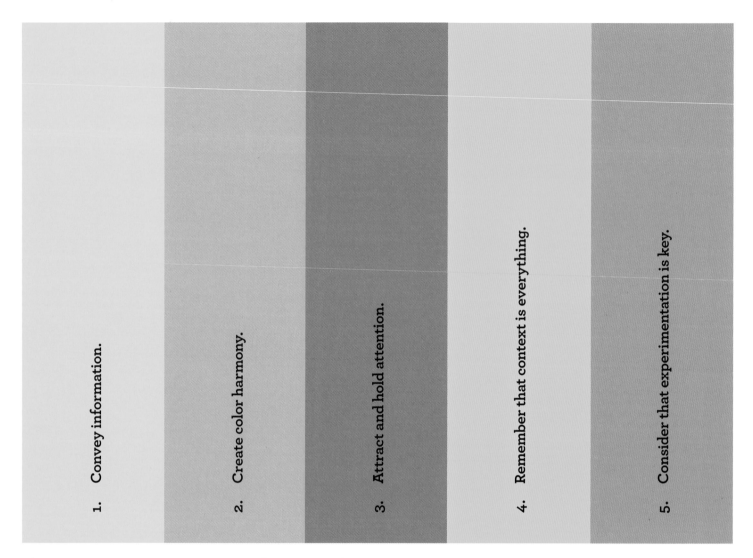

1. Convey information.

2. Create color harmony.

3. Attract and hold attention.

4. Remember that context is everything.

5. Consider that experimentation is key.

**Chapter 4**

# 10 Rules of Color

There really are no right or wrong ways to use color. Some color design processes and color combinations work better than others, but there are many ways to achieve great results. Following are ten rules as a way to approach color. The rules incorporate physics, theory, psychology, economics, aesthetics, and usage in order to effectively harness this powerful design element.

6. Know that people see color differently.

7. Assist in mnemonic value.

8. Think about composition.

9. Use standardized color systems.

10. Understand limitations.

# 1   Convey Information

**The Right Color Sends the Right Message**

Color has the ability to evoke a response, create a mood, symbolize an idea, and express an emotion. Differences in particular aspects of color, such as a change in value or intensity, can further refine a color's tone and meaning. People have their own associations with color, but there are conscious and subconscious social and cultural connotations too. Every color has its own set of connections that convey information, with the color itself acting as a signifier of ideas—both positive and negative. (See Color Meaning, Chapter 3.)

**Sources of Color Meanings**

All color meanings are relative; these interpretations are influenced by a variety of factors, including age, gender, personal experience, mood, ethnic identity, history, and tradition. Affinity for the particular colors of a nation's flag shows how tradition, nationalism, and history impact color responses.

Color preferences that predominate when a person comes of age (or nostalgia for a particular time in history) can cause resonance. For example, the earth-tone palette of harvest gold, avocado green, and burnt orange—central to 1970s color schemes—evokes strong associations in people who were teenagers then.

Color assignment based on gender, as in the Western tradition of pink for girls and blue for boys, is both adopted and subverted in children's products. However, it is rare for male-oriented objects to be colored pink in any culture. Are such differences between the sexes due to physiology or socialization? No one is quite sure, but a recent study found that more women than men have a favorite color. Also, when asked for a preference between bright and soft colors, women tend to pick soft colors while men choose bright ones.

Age is another important factor related to color interpretation. Children and the elderly have an affinity for intense, bright colors. Teenagers like whatever their parents don't appreciate. In addition, a 1976 study showed the effects of color on mood. Groups of people were placed in different rooms—one colorful and complex, the other gray and sterile. Researchers recorded pulse rates as well as individuals' subjective emotional feelings. The results showed stress and boredom in the gray room, supporting the notion that color causes both physical and emotional responses, all of which could trigger judgments about specific colors.

**Tapping into Color's Associations**

Psychologists have suggested that color impression can account for as much as 60 percent of the acceptance or rejection of a product or service. When choosing colors to enhance the message being communicated, it is essential to anticipate audience perceptions. All color is relative, and people can have strong, often subconscious, prejudices against certain colors and color schemes.

It is a designer's job to select colors that elicit correct responses. They need to consider carefully for whom a piece is being created, and how internal and external audiences will read the design in terms of color alone. It's not just an aesthetic choice. Designers need to leverage color meaning to achieve their client's goals.

In the poster for an AIGA event and lecture, the red, white, and blue, Wonder Bread, and American flag relays the "All-American" reputation of Sean Adams, the speaker. The irreverent use of these colors and addition of yellow leverages this concept while gently lampooning it, using imagery and color to echo the theme.
**Sean Adams**

More than just a visual phenomenon, color has emotional and cultural dimensions that can enhance—or impede—communication efforts.

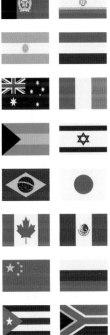

Right: A representative sample of flags from countries around the world. Designers can take cues from these color palettes to create affinity, as well as discord, with their designs. Nationalism is often strongly associated with flag colors and is therefore a key factor in inherent color meaning for many people.

Left: The color scheme of red and black supports the passionate emotional content of the play *Fucking A* which is promoted in this New York Public Theater poster designed by Paula Scher and Sean Carmody. *Fucking A* is Suzan-Lori Park's contemporary reshaping of the classic novel *The Scarlet Letter*. Today, the *A* stands for abortion rather than for adultery. Wearing red letters was a public source of shame in colonial America, and the designers employ this concept and color convention in the poster for the play.
**Pentagram**

"Research reveals that all human beings make an unconscious judgment about a person, environment, or item within ninety seconds of initial viewing and that between 62 percent and 90 percent of that assessment is based on color alone."—**The Institute for Color Research**

Art+Com worked with the O2 cell phone company when it opened the first German flagship store in the city of Munich. The central feature of the store is an 18-meter long interactive, intensely colored, multimedia strip. Along the entire length of the sensory strip customers are able to call up detailed information on products, services and offers. The installation winds its way through the room on various levels, starting as an interactive floor projection and flowing into a tabletop before becoming a wall projection.
**Art+Com**

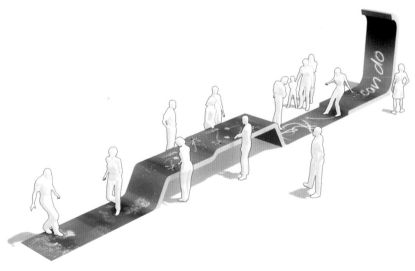

Is there a difference in the way males and females respond to and interpret color? Yes. Some of the research leads us to wonder whether it is nature or nurture. Regardless, the gender of the intended audience is an important factor to consider when choosing a color palette for any design project. A 1934 study found evidence that the most pleasing color combinations were obtained from either very small or very large differences in hue, rather than medium differences. The small differences were more frequently preferred by females than males. Based on this information, perhaps females can discern more differences in colors than males.

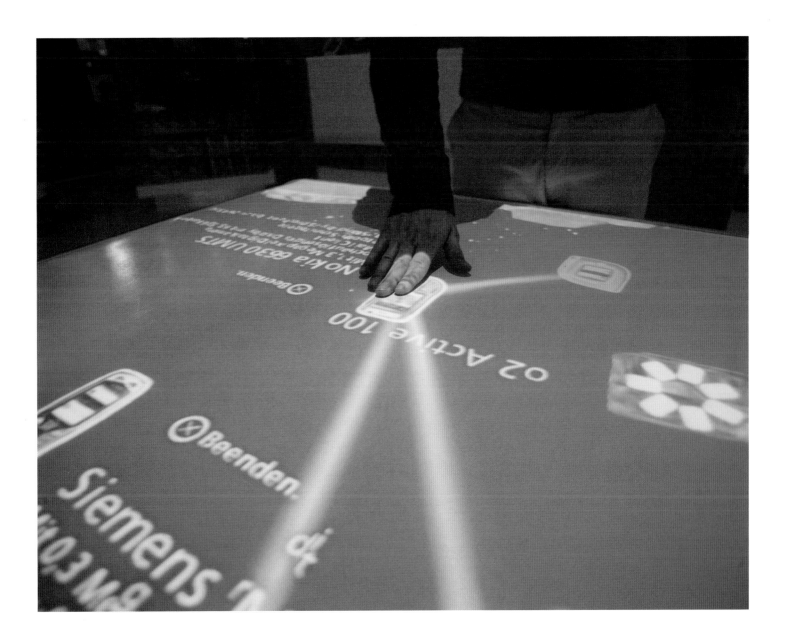

In a 1959 study, researchers found that males were generally more tolerant of achromatic colors (colors with zero saturation and, therefore, no hue, such as neutral grays, white, or black) than females. This led researchers to propose that females might be more color-conscious as well as more flexible and diverse in their color preferences.

Researchers also found in a 1990 study that females are more likely than males to have a favorite color. When asked whether they preferred light versus dark colors, there were no significant differences between males and females. However, when asked to choose between bright or soft colors, the females preferred soft colors, while the

males preferred the bright ones. What is the favorite color of each gender? There is no one answer—research seems to provide conflicting results. Another study of color identification and vocabulary was done with college students in 1995. Students were asked to look at and identify twenty-one different color chips. The Females recognized

**Using Proprietary Colors to Convey Information**

The idea of "owning" a color is one of the highest priorities in managing logos and corporate identities and is generally important to all design and advertising visual systems. Orange has been associated with the children's television network Nickelodeon for almost two decades. Pantone 655, a deep, dark blue, is used in the identity system of retail clothing giant The Gap and was also the name of one of the company's fragrance products. In these cases, color creates a symbolic link with the producer and its products. A bright golden yellow has been associated with photographic products manufacturer Kodak for decades. The color becomes a stand-in for the concepts of "kids' entertainment" or "trendy clothing" or even arguably, "photography."

Perhaps subverting standard meanings would help to make a color proprietary. What if a health-related product had a black or brown logo instead of the expected green one? Would organic food packaging jump off the shelf more if it were designed in unnatural, even day-glo, colors? What about a slick, high-tech company adopting an earthy organic color palette? All of these could separate a brand from its competition. Most clients would relish the idea of having color alone symbolize their company.

**Color as a Convention**

Color meanings are held deep in our subconscious. Color is a state of mind as much as anything. In a physical sense, there is no such thing as color, just light waves of different wavelengths. The human eye can distinguish between the wavelengths, so we see the world in color. However, the human brain perceives more. We *feel* color. It has biological, psychological, social, and cultural dimensions, all of which give it meaning and convey information.

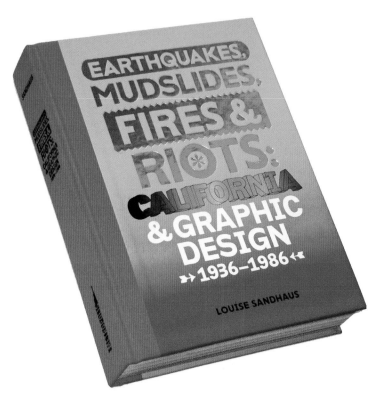

Louise Sandhaus' design for her book, *Earthquakes, Mudslides, Fires & Riots: California & Graphic Design 1936-1986* introduces fluorescent yellow and pink to a pastel and metallic palette. The combination, according to classical color theory, should clash. But in this instance they work harmoniously conveying the casual California lifestyle, sunsets, and surf culture. The unapologetic and bold choice mirrors California design's radical reputation. **Louise Sandhaus**

significantly more elaborate colors than the males. Findings also indicated that the differences in responses to color identification might be attributed to a difference in the way males and females are socialized.

"Colors are the mother tongue of the subconscious."—**Carl Jung**

When Aiwa became a subsidiary of Sony Corporation, the consumer electronics brand repositioned itself to create stylish and innovative audio/video products for the youth market. Hello Design, in partnership with Weiden + Kennedy, The_Groop, and Oceanmonsters, designed and developed Aiwaworld TV, the main portion of Aiwaworld to serve up audiovisual "hybrid music." Above are four screens featuring the colorful animated world created for Aiwaworld TV. The designers used a parallax engine to create a 3-D experience in which users can explore a topsy-turvy world inspired by Japanese pop culture. A bright palette of colors echoes the comic book references, working to fully immerse the viewer in a kinder, more fun-filled world. No dominant color is used to convey a particular message in Aiwaworld TV; rather, it is a collection of colors taken from the Japanese anime genre, which has a youthful voice. The colors work to invite the viewer into a familiar yet new kind of storytelling. Aiwaworld TV not only complements existing Aiwaworld content but also provides an engaging experience that speaks to young audiences, creating a unique brand impression for the client. **Hello Design**

# 2    Create Color Harmony

To a certain extent, pleasing color harmony is just like any other aspect of beauty: it is in the eye of the beholder. What is pleasing to one person may not be pleasing to another. Color harmony nevertheless is related to the organizing principles of all artwork: balance, variety, proportion, dominance, movement, rhythm, and repetition. These are some of the traditional metrics for determining whether or not a piece, be it fine art or graphic design, is pleasing and works.

## Making Color Choices

Keeping this in mind, designers need to select the colors for each and every project carefully. Some of their decisions may be based on their own preferences, while others may be heavily influenced by client input and preferences. Selecting inventive combinations of hues, along with specific tints and shades, is a practiced skill. The more you do it, the better you get.

Most designers seek a color scheme that engages the viewer and provides a balanced visual experience. The deliberate avoidance of harmony must be viewed as a means of inducing an agitated or chaotic reaction in the viewer. Designers must decide in what direction they are headed and for what reason. The starting point for all decisions about color harmony comes down to a creative interpretation of the message that needs to be communicated. What combination of colors will best convey the desired meaning? If those colors are clichéd and overused, what are the best alternatives? Can the effect be refined by a slight modification of color choice?

Ferro-Concrete's design for *The LA Downtowner* reveals insider views of Downtown LA's food, drinks, culture and the people who shape it. New businesses advertise their events and offerings, putting their business in front of the sought-after audience of younger, lifestyle driven influencers they need to thrive. The color palette of fresh and clear colors invites the user into the information. This palette is contrary to the perception that downtown Los Angeles is gray and dismal.
**Ferro-Concrete**

Harmony is a factor of cohesion—the pleasing relationships among graphic elements, especially color.

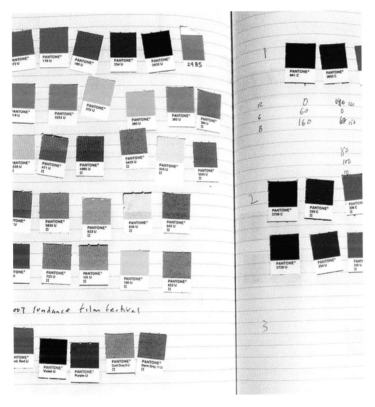

## Eight Rules for Building a Color Palette

The following steps are recommended for creating timeless color schemes that are effective in all media and for all cultures. The steps are based on the research of Professor Hideaki Chijiwa, Musashino Bijutsu Daigaku (Musashino University of Fine Arts), in the book *Color Harmony: A Guide to Creative Color Combinations* (Rockport Publishers).

### 1. Figure out the purpose.
Think about why you are choosing a color palette and for what kind of client. Investigate color meanings and associations.

### 2. Review color basics.
Make sure you have reviewed basics such as hue, saturation, intensity, and the ways in which colors affect each other in relationship. Study layouts you like to analyze possible palettes for the current project.

### 3. Choose a dominant color, accent colors.
Decide on an overall background color, or color for the largest areas, first. Then select possible accent colors. Sometimes the accent color is fixed. For example, a client may have a corporate color that must be used. In that case, keep the accent color in mind when selecting the dominant color.

### 4. Select shades, then vary them.
Because the shade of a color impacts the overall impression, decide what feeling must be conveyed—bright and cheery, or perhaps serene and dignified. Note that colors of the same hue but of varying shades and tints can look different and still remain harmonious. Varying the shades of hues creates contrast and can be effective and dramatic.

### 5. Look at compatibility of hues.
Having selected a preliminary color scheme and considered a variety of tints and shades, look at the overall compatibility of colors. Is the contrast pleasing? If not, go back to refine the palette with intermediate hues. For example, with green selected as the dominant color, perhaps red-orange would work better than pure red.

### 6. Limit the number of colors.
With a palette now chosen, review the number of colors. Two or three colors are usually enough. Four must be chosen with care, while five might be too many. Sometimes budget limitations as well as aesthetic considerations narrow the palette.

### 7. Put the colors into action.
Put the colors to use in a few typical pieces required by the client. Look at how they work together. If the color palette is successful, your designs will be harmonious. If not, further refinements are warranted.

### 8. Keep a logbook.
Once you have found color palettes that work, document them in a journal. Paste in color chips and include the client's name and a project description. The logbook will serve as a reference when choosing future color palettes.

Sean Adams keeps a notebook of color palettes as an easy reference guide to color schemes. Above, see pages for the Sundance Film Festival and ArtCenter Graduate Viewbook color palettes.

This logbook of ideas includes approved and unapproved color palettes and serves as a creative resource for thinking about color in all types of projects. **Sean Adams**

PANTONE Colors displayed here may not match the PANTONE-identified standards. Consult current PANTONE Color Publications for accurate color. PANTONE® and the PANTONE Chip Logo® are the property of Pantone, Inc.

## Combining Colors

The science of color harmony involves the categorization and determination of the dynamic symmetry in color groupings. Effectively doing so goes back to understanding and utilizing color theory to create color relationships such as complements, split complements, triads, analogies, and monochromatic. (Please see Chapter 2.) Color science becomes art when a designer knows how to use colors, in what proportions, and for what purpose, to create a response.

Designers know that contrast intensifies color. Fully saturated colors create a lively impression. White and black alter the perception of other colors. Different types of color schemes have different positive and negative factors. For example, analogous color schemes (adjacent hues on the color wheel) are soothing to the eye and easy to create but lack contrast and vibrancy. Split complementary color schemes (a hue plus the two hues adjacent to its complement) are more sophisticated and nuanced than complementary color schemes (two hues

directly opposite on the color wheel). Split complements have a strong visual impact but can be difficult to balance. Triadic color schemes (three hues equally spaced around the color wheel) offer contrast, but less contrast than a complementary scheme. Tetradic, or double complementary color schemes (two pairs of complementary hues), are the richest schemes with the most variety but are by far the hardest to balance. Monochromatic color schemes (variations in tints and shades of a single hue) are clean and elegant but lack contrast and often lack impact as well.

Naturally, there are always exceptions. Talented, creative people can take delight in stretching the boundaries of what works in color schemes. Color harmony fascinates designers. Experimenting with it allows them to develop their unique point of view. Color interactions are both optical and aesthetic phenomena. Designers must formulate a process for visualizing color combinations that allows them to shift with changing media, clients, and trends in color usage.

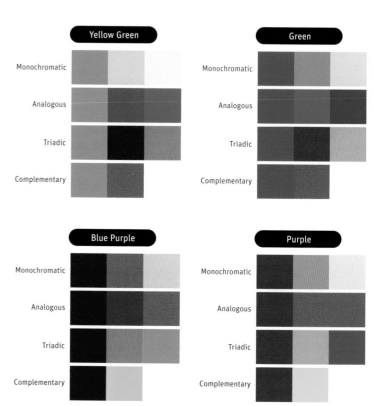

"Besides a balance through color harmony, which is comparable
to symmetry, there is equilibrium between color tensions,
related to a more dynamic equilibrium." —Josef Albers

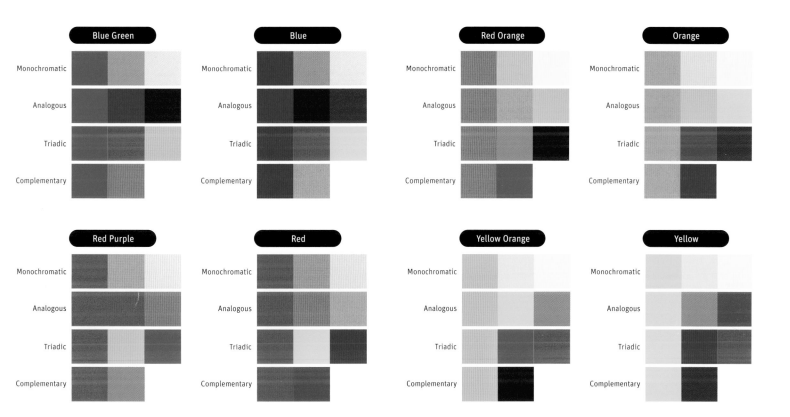

## Color Harmony Chart

Shown here is a reference guide for creating pleasing color harmonies. Included for each of the hues of the twelve-step color wheel is an example of a monochromatic, analogous, triadic, and complementary color scheme. These samples can be used as a reminder of possible color combinations when beginning the process of building a color scheme for a project. Color harmony is often a fusion of the fundamentals of color physics tempered by aesthetic practice. Color can be used to dazzle, soothe, charm, irritate, agitate, or annoy—all through the choice of specific relationships.

**Color on a Biological Level**

Chromotherapy, or color therapy, is a practice that uses the seven colors of the rainbow spectrum to promote health and healing. It is based on the premise that certain colors are infused with certain specific healing energies.

Color has played a role in healing for different cultures. In ancient Egypt, people were treated in rooms designed specifically to refract the sun's rays into different colors of the visible spectrum. Practitioners of Ayurveda, especially in India, believe that specific colors correspond with each of the seven chakras, or energy centers, of the body.

Traditional Chinese medicine holds that each organ of the body is associated with a certain color. In Qigong, a self-healing art that combines movement and meditation, different organs and emotions are associated with both healing sounds and specific colors. Both practices use color to treat a wide variety of mental and physical imbalances. In 1878, physician Edwin D. Babbitt (1828–1905) published *Principles of Light and Color,* in which he described his work on healing with colored lights. Though controversial, Babbitt's work continues to inspire color therapists today.

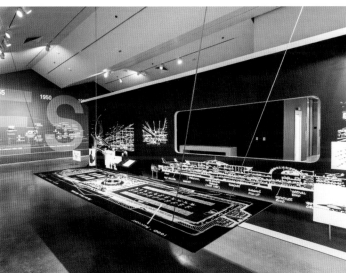

**Modernist Maverick:**
**The Architecture of William L. Pereira.**
*Nevada Museum of Art,*
*Reno, Nevada*

Nik Hafermaas' design for an interpretative exhibition surveys the architecture, urban planning, and design work of William L. Pereira. The structures Pereira designed were large in scale, ranging from San Francisco's iconic Transamerica Tower to the Los Angeles County Museum of Art and from San Diego Geisel Library to the master plan for California's Irvine Ranch and the Los Angeles International Airport (LAX).

The exhibition design uses color and form to be as bold as Pereira's future-forward form language, that oscillates between refinement and visual drama. From the Transamerica stalactite sculpture in the grand atrium and the perforated cocoon surrounding Pereira's personal life, to the succession of Panavision frames celebrating models of his most iconic buildings; the entire exhibition is a play of color, scale, and cinematic vistas that invite the audience to discover and to physically engage.
**Uberall**

# 3 Attract and Hold Attention

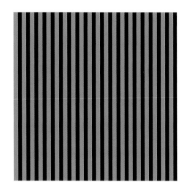

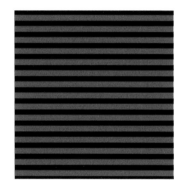

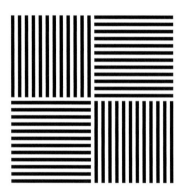

As color is a visual language in and of itself, a designer can use it to attract the eye and focus attention on the intended messages in the work. Color can be used to irritate or relax, encourage participation or alienate—it is completely up to the designer. Josef Albers said, "Whether bright or dull, singular or complex, physiological or psychological, theoretical or experiential, the persuasive power of color attracts and motivates."

## Color Physiology Influences Design

Strong visual statements can distinguish a designer's work and the client's message from the competition. Using physiological phenomena to get attention will also assist in this goal. Our brains and eyes participate with the designer to either accept or reject a particular design. As humans, we seek balance, especially in terms of color. For example, when exposed to a particular hue, our brains seem to expect the complementary color. If it is present, the combination looks vibrant. If it is absent, our brains tend to produce it to form a balance.

The eye naturally recognizes certain contrasts and colors, specifically the colors found in the rainbow spectrum. Perception of other colors, such as muted tertiary colors and tints and shades of spectrum hues, may require an intellectual shift to recognize. Since humans cannot see all possible colors, color perception is evoked by picking up on dominant wavelengths of spectral light. Dominant wavelength is the perceptual idea that gives us the concept of hue (e.g., if the dominant wavelength of an object is red, the object is perceived as being the color red). Therefore, the eye is nearly always drawn to what it can easily perceive. This is the scientific reason why a design utilizing primary colors attracts our attention instantly.

## Optical Illusions Can Affect Design

Fascinating insights into how humans perceive and interpret color can be gained by studying optical illusions. Although we don't have a complete model of the way color information gets processed by the eye and brain, scientific research offers glimpses of various phenomena that can prove significant to our understanding of

This optical illusion is known as the McCollough Effect. Look at the colored grids, above, for a few minutes. Then look at the black and white grids. There should seem to be a green haze around the horizontal lines and a magenta haze around the vertical lines. The McCollough Effect demonstrates that color and orientation are two sources of stimulation in humans. Designers must consider not only the particular colors they choose but also their physical relationships, which affect perception. This effect demonstrates how our eyes and brains seek the complements of colors by creating the sensation of them.

Leveraging the way the eye and brain respond to color physiologically, while linking it to emotional and aesthetic considerations, will help to attract and hold the viewer's attention.

how color works in design compositions. Visualizations of certain color combinations often play tricks on us, as illustrated in the diagrams on these pages.

Scientists have studied color, and their research can be helpful to designers. Colors react to each other on many levels, so it is important for a designer to understand this and leverage it.

**The Transparency Effect**
Another perceptual phenomenon that can add to color compositions in design, especially in terms of creating special illusions, is called the Transparency Effect.

In color mixing, designers seek relationships between colors by combining hues to create a specific hue. When two hues are mixed to form a third, the resulting color resembles both. If placed between the original two, the new mixed hue will not only be harmonious, but will also give the illusion of transparency.

This chart shows the Munker-White Effect. Even though the blue bars are identical, when surrounded by different colors such as white or black, they appear to be completely different hues. This optical illusion also demonstrates a method for obtaining the appearance of more colors in a layout.

In cases shown above, the original two colors look like overlapped transparent sheets that form the new middle color. These types of optical phenomena can be utilized to draw the eye into a design by achieving harmony and concordance among all the colors present.

This poster for a performance of the Stockholm Improvisational Theater attracts attention with a bold use of color and shape. The dark indigo-blue juxtaposed with a near-complementary yellow-orange and white creates the optical illusion of depth.
**Sweden Graphics**

"One way to make yourself stand out from the crowd is by using color in ways nobody else thought of."—**Josef Albers**

Aesthetically, Stefan Bücher set out to make the book, *344 Questions*, as fun and usable as possible. It's a small format, so the reader can carry it like a sketchbook. The flexi-binding makes it sturdy without being heavy. The gradations of bright colors create a book that invites the reader and makes it fun to look at and fill out.

**344 Design**

Another example of the way color interactions alter perception and get attention are these two vehicle colors for Optimum., a cable, internet and voice service throughout New York, New Jersey, and the West. The unadorned brand identity program captures the straightforwardness of the brand. The simple and vibrant colors work together to create a proprietary voice while maintaining variety.

**Collins**

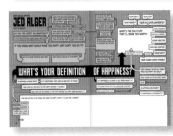

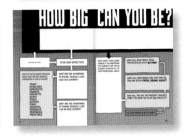

### After-imaging, A Color Perception Phenomenon

Another interesting color perception phenomenon is called after-imaging. Every color has an opposite, or complement. It is possible to determine a color's complement just by using our eyes. The rods and cones in our eyes vary in sensitivity to different light and will fatigue after prolonged exposure to a hue. Once fatigued, we will perceive the complement of that hue when we look away.

You can try this for yourself. Look at the flag image for several minutes, then gaze at a white sheet—you are experiencing an afterimage. Now stare at the blue square at right. After a few minutes, look at the gray square above it. You should be able to see a square of the blue's complement—orange.

After-imaging and other optical illusions are noteworthy because designers must understand that colors can significantly alter each other when juxtaposed.

## Color and Human Emotion

Color is used in various forms of alternative medicine; color psychology is one example. This field, a relatively new area of research, is devoted to analyzing the effects that color has on human emotion. Some may call it a pseudoscience, but color psychology has its devotees worldwide.

Practitioners of color psychology, which is related to chromotherapy, note that many common physiological effects often accompany psychological responses to certain colors. However, variables such as age and cultural background may also affect responses.

Color psychology is of particular significance to environmental graphic designers, whose color choices for installations and environments can affect people's mood and actions. Color is an active influence on human consciousness.

Color has an impact on us because every cell in the body responds to light, and color is light. So we react to it, literally, on a cellular level. Color affects our bodies, our minds, and our moods.

Color can be used in a cityscape to attract attention. The large format banners for the BALTIC Centre for Contemporary Art in northern England are a striking combination of black and yellow. The color scheme evokes heavy industry as well as modern art. **blue river design**

Based on research of a typical retail environment, color was used to differentiate a new line of Stanley automotive parts. In a strategic attempt to draw attention away from other products, a vivid burnt orange was chosen as the new core color for the brand. **Hornall Anderson Design Works**

# 4 Remember That Context Is Everything

Color is always seen in context. Sometimes that context is proximity to another color, which alters its meaning or even the perception of the color itself. At other times the context is the environment surrounding the color—for example, the white of a page or the physical environment as a whole. The perception of color is always shifting, never fixed. All colors appear more brilliant when set against a black background. Conversely, they seem a bit duller on a white background. Complementary colors make each other appear brighter, yet the effect on the brain, when taken in total, is a balanced neutral gray. Certain color triadic schemes seem more garish or more sophisticated, more lively, or more sedate.

## All Color Is Relative

The constant experimentation that occurs in the design process brings to light which colors are most pleasing to a particular designer's eyes. By understanding that all color is relative, designers can observe for themselves the effects colors have on each other. Sometimes a slight variation in tint or shade is enough to create the required emotional and aesthetic feeling.

## Proximity to Other Colors

Optical color mixing, also referred to as *partitive color or simultaneous contrast,* is another important contextual phenomenon. This is the color perception that results from the combination of adjacent color areas by the eye and brain. Human perception mixes colors that are next to each other and forms a color impression based on the entire composition. The viewer may perceive colors that are not actually present. If it is imperative that a specific color is perceived first by the viewer, be sure to keep this phenomenon in mind.

In addition, a hue's position on the color wheel can affect the perception of other hues. Hues that are next to each other have an easier relationship than those that are opposite each other, which results in active complementary contrast. The concept of the advancing and receding natures of colors must also be considered. Warm colors always advance and seem nearer, while cool ones recede and seem more distant.

Designers can achieve an optical fluttering of the edges of the colors in their layouts, creating an impression of lively movement. Alternatively, they can make transitions nearly invisible and ease the flow of the eye by using more harmoniously related colors. Juxtapositions of colors cause interactions, enhancing or distracting from the intended message. Proximity literally changes the character of a color. All of these context-related aspects of color can be utilized to either the advantage or the detriment of a design. Success is a matter of the intent of the piece and the skill of the designer.

## Environmental Influences Change Color Perception

The end use of the piece—its particular medium—must be considered as well. A design for a retail environment involves different considerations than a design for television broadcast, for example. Both applications require that the design be seen, be understood, and communicate a given message. However, the color considerations may be totally different.

A retail product package color is probably chosen in relation to other products—if every other competitor is pink and purple, then perhaps orange is a better choice. The color helps the product stand out. This is an example of the context influencing the concept as well as creating an idea that is context specific.

Lambeth First is a partnership of community groups south of London. Different color combinations represent a variety of voices, allowing color to express a multicultural context.
**Atelier Works**

"A color has many faces."—**Josef Albers**

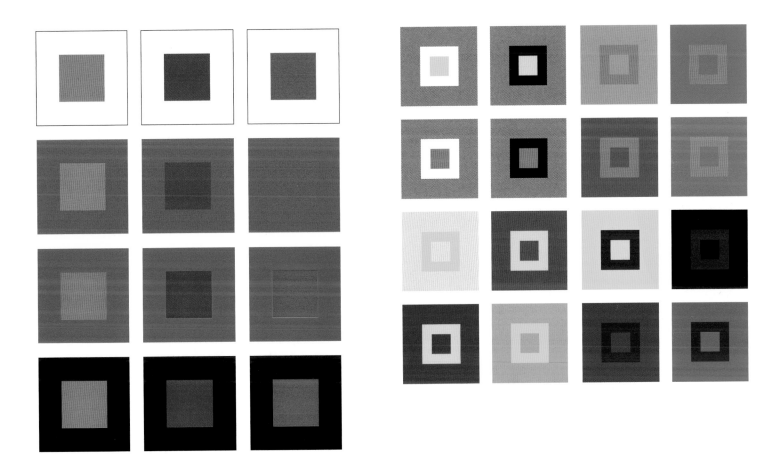

A study in color contrasts—three different red squares, each with its own vertical column, are set on the same color backgrounds—white, red, green, and black. Note how the colors shift in relation to each other. Colors mutually influence each other, altering perception.

Provocative color effects can be achieved with very slight variations in hue, as demonstrated here.

An illustration of color effects—how one color impacts another. Notice how the same yellow and blues look very different on the various background colors. Some combinations vibrate, some are soothing. Although the colors are used in equal amounts, some combinations make the middle squares look larger or smaller. Colors can be completely altered in expression by different juxtapositions or different contexts.

**The Science of Color Comparison**

Several German scientists and artists have noticed, researched, and written about the laws of chromatic contrast as well as the active role of the brain in the development of color relationships and perceptions.

Johann von Wolfgang Goethe greatly advanced color research. He was one of the first to draw attention to and describe the phenomena that can accompany colors in contrast to one another. He is most famous, however, for his approach to the treatment of color. He argued that light,

shade, and hue are associated with emotional experience. His unorthodox theories of the character of light and color influenced abstract painters such as Wassily Kandinsky and Piet Mondrian. Another influential thinker about color interaction was German physicist and meteorologist Johann Friedrich Wilhelm von Bezold (1837–1907). His

## Light affects color

Color is light, but light also affects color. Whether it is the depiction of a real-world scene in a color illustration or the calculation of how a colored graphic may appear in its actual usage location, illumination is a factor that the designer must understand.

To create the illusion of depth in a particular piece, a designer may wish to show shadows when one form overlaps another. Whether cast by single or multiple light sources, shadows are commonly approximated by creating a shape that includes some of the complement of the original color. Also, warm light tends to cast a cold shadow, and vice versa.

Another aspect of color and light is color constancy—the tendency in human perception that allows us to compensate for various conditions and types of illumination. Color constancy is a psychophysical response that lets us recognize colors,

and therefore objects, no matter what the light is like—whether it is low or bright, fluorescent, natural, or incandescent. We see an object as a certain hue because it reflects more of a particular wavelength of a specific color of light— so a tangerine looks orange because it reflects more orange light than other objects near it. Further, due to color constancy, that tangerine will seem orange to us in bright sunlight or by candlelight in a darkened room because our visual system compensates for changing illumination.

Chromatic adaptation allows for changes in environments as well. This is demonstrated when a person walks from full sunlight into a building. At first, the environment seems very dark, then our eyes gradually adapt, and true colors become apparent. Our eyes and brains are constantly adjusting to varying light conditions.

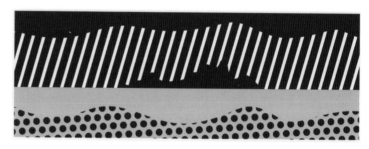

professional expertise was the physics of the atmosphere, especially electrical storms, but his contribution to color physics came from his hobby—rug making. Bezold's uncle, Gustav, was a prominent art historian, which also may have influenced his foray into color research. Bezold noticed that certain strong colors, when evenly distributed, entirely changed the effect of his rug designs. This effect is now known as the Bezold Effect. He is also known for the Bezold-Brücke Phenomenon, which is the changing perception of colors under the effects of increased light intensity; in other words, the apparent brightness of hues changes as illumination changes.

A series of three full-page illustrations that accompany a *Raket* magazine article on the human fascination with islands. Nonrepresentational colors are used, stepping away from a natural color scheme. Color is used to create an abstraction of the idea of islands. The series shows that varying the color palettes in this context causes changes in the reading of images that are structurally similar.
**Sweden Graphics**

**Simultaneous Contrast**

One of the important early studies of the science of color harmony was done by French chemist Michel Eugène Chevreul (1786–1889). Chevreul introduced a systematic approach to seeing colors in his 1839 *De la loi du contraste simultané des couleurs et de l'assortiment des objets colorés* (published in English as *The Principles of Harmony and Contrast of Colors*). The book is both historically and aesthetically significant.

Chevreul was appointed the director of dyeing at the Manufacture Royale des Gobelins (the Gobelins Royal Tapestry Works) in 1824. He came to realize that many of the problems encountered in the firm's weaving had to do with how and which colors affected each other. His findings, set forth in

**The Relativity of Color**

Josef Albers was a German artist and educator. He was one of the original teachers in the Bauhaus who emigrated to the U.S. and was responsible for major innovations in art education. As an artist, Albers is best known for his series of abstract paintings *Homage to a Square;* as a color theorist, he is known for his book *Interaction of Color,* published in 1963.

Albers's work demonstrates that "a color has many faces." He explored the subtle relationships among colors, and his methods of studying and teaching allow artists and designers to discover these relationships for themselves through a series of practical exercises. Among the principles Albers sought to illustrate are positive and reversed grounds (what happens when the colors of the feature elements and the backgrounds are exchanged), transparency effects, spatial relationships (how to create the optical illusion of depth), vibrating and vanishing boundaries, and proportional variances. In addition, he demonstrated how all of these affect art and design.

In *Interaction of Color,* Albers takes the reader through a series of experiments, such as the one illustrated below, right, that lead to knowledge and understanding of color relationships. These exercises, too numerous and in-depth to explore here, can be used by designers to teach themselves more about color in a hands-on manner, and we recommend doing so. The Albers course, often taught in design schools, helps designers recognize and develop their own inclinations and aptitude with color.

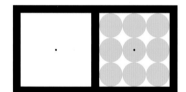

One of Albers' many experiments to show the illusion of double or reversed after-imaging, often called contrast reversal, is illustrated here. Look at the yellow circles, at left, for a minute. Now shift your eyes quickly to the left square. You might expect to see the complement of yellow. However, yellow diamond shapes, mirroring the negative space between the circles, appear instead.

Context became inspiration for the identity for Slade Gardens, a community adventure playground. Experiencing the park, designer Ian Childers noticed his children, dressed in bright red clothing, enjoying the elaborate green play structures. This observation resulted in the logo and its signage application.
**Atelier Works**

his book, deal with simultaneous contrast. Simultaneous contrast is a form of color mixing referred to as *medial*. This color mixing is how our eyes and brains combine colors that are next to each other to form a particular color impression. Chevreul's work on the physics of color and color effects had a great impact on the world of art. Particularly affected were the Neo-impressionists, especially the Pointillist painters Georges Seurat and Paul Signac.

In a busy, cluttered context, such as the ITC Telecom World Trade Show in Geneva, the HP Telecom booth stands out. Colors from the new HP palette were used to delineate content areas within the booth. As it was the first trade show to showcase HP's new look and feel, the color scheme served a dual purpose: as navigation to help visitors find the areas and topics they were interested in, and as a way to bring the corporate colors to life in three dimensions, signaling the emergence of the new HP brand.
**Stone Yamashita Partners**

# **5** Consider That Experimentation Is Key

Experimenting with color challenges a designer's imagination and often results in a variety of unexpected new solutions. This can work through changing contrast, volume, and proportion; stretching conventional notions of color harmony; or altering color temperature.

Allowing one color to dominate, in contrast to others, focuses attention on design elements in that color and allows them to communicate a distinct message. Layouts that feature strong contrasts between colors in terms of hue, saturation, and value have the greatest possibilities for expressive effect. However, designers must work to unify the contrasting elements without destroying the strength and impact of the piece.

Adjusting volume or proportion of each color used can provide interesting results. For example, a small—dark spot of color, because it is of lower value, can dominate a large light area. Proportion can be used by incorporating a large area of a light hue. Conversely, large amounts of dark values make the design appear dark, even somber. Alternating color based on saturation rather than proportion completely changes the perceived visual mix of color.

"Why do two colors, put next to each other, sing?
Can we really explain this? No." —**Pablo Picasso**

The New Yorker Festival 2016 is an annual festival with talks, interviews, screenings and performances from the worlds of film, fiction, politics, comedy, science, fashion, food, and more. Creative director Todd St. John used a pattern of colored blocks to convey the grid of Manhattan streets, except Broadway, running on an angle. The sophisticated palette matches The New Yorker's intellectual brand without appearing dull and uninteresting.
**Hunter Gatherer**

This chart illustrates two types of dominance. *Contrast dominance*, seen in the vertical series of squares on the left, shows that contrast increases with levels of intensity or saturation. On the right, *value dominance* is shown in three compositions: first, all tints; then pure hues; and, finally, all shades.

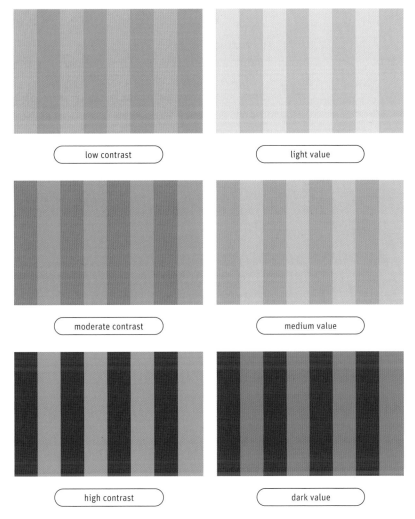

low contrast

light value

moderate contrast

medium value

high contrast

dark value

## Ideas for Experimentation

There are many approaches to the idea of experimenting with color. Sometimes looking at the process from a slightly new perspective can add life and freshness to a designer's work. Here are things to consider:

- Use a restricted palette; impose your own limits on the range of colors.
- Try using colors you dislike to see if you can make a pleasing arrangement.
- Use only your favorite colors.
- Deliberately aim for concord or, alternatively, for discord.
- Choose pairs of contrasting colors.
- Subordinate your own choice of colors and work only with the client's preferences.
- Vary the scale of color usage. Allow for dominance.
- Design by choosing a mood for the piece first.
- Choose colors before shapes.
- Alter the rhythm and flow of your colors to see what happens.
- Always echo your colors. Repetition causes harmony.
- Look to the masters of fine arts, such as your favorite painter, and utilize their palettes.

**Color in Professional Sports**

Colors are chosen by sports teams and approved by their respective leagues. Designers and marketing experts often weigh in on the decision as well because team merchandise is big business. Colors are kept simple to translate for marketing and advertising purposes. Fashion trends seem to affect choice. Most important, colors must look good in motion when the athletes are playing. Intense colors capture the kinetic energy of sport. In theory, team colors add a psychological edge to the team's performance. According to a Cornell University study analyzing the penalty records of twenty-eight National Football League teams from 1970 to 1986, four teams wearing black uniforms were

**The Power of Contrast**

Exploring the notion of contrast is an effective experimentation tool. Contrast is the perceived difference between adjacent colors in a design. The highest levels of contrast appear between the achromatic colors—black and white. Complementary colors also have high chromatic contrast. Contrast levels allow for aesthetic expression and determine legibility.

The famed color theorist Johannes Itten observed the following seven types of contrast:

**1**

**2**

**3**

**The contrast of hue:**
the juxtaposition of colors at their most intense.

**Light-dark contrast:**
formed by juxtaposition of light and dark values, including those in monochromatic compositions.

**Cold-warm contrast:**
juxtaposition of hues that are considered warm or cool. Three-dimensional depth occurs with this contrast because of the advancing (warm) and receding (cool) characteristics.

among the most penalized. Similarly, the three most penalized National Hockey League teams during that same time period wore black. These findings indicate that black may be the color associated with the most aggressive sports teams. Our informal look at U.S. professional sports teams finds that the top four colors in order of frequency of use are: Basketball: blue, red, yellow/gold, and black; Football: blue, black, red, and yellow/gold; Baseball: blue, red, and black, with yellow/gold a distant fourth; and Hockey: blue and red, with black and yellow/gold tied for third. Interestingly, the colors for each sport are the same, but the order of frequency differs.

**4**

**5**

**6**

**7**

**Complementary contrast:**
the juxtaposition of hues opposite each other on the color wheel.

**Simultaneous contrast:**
the contrast formed when adjacent hue boundaries perceptually vibrate as they optically mix.

**The contrast of saturation:**
the juxtaposition of more and less saturated colors.

**The contrast of extension, also called the contrast of proportion:**
formed by assigning proportional field sizes in relation to the visual weight of a hue.

"Color is a means of exerting a direct influence on the soul." —**Wassily Kandinsky**

The *IF/THEN* book about digital technology was designed to incorporate a sense of discovery and play. A variety of large-format black-and-white images are contrasted with rich color fields that are supplied by the insertion of different-colored paper stocks or printed as large areas of solid color. Display type in large point sizes contrasts with pages of smaller book type. Experimentation with scale, contrast, and color humanizes the high-tech subject of the book and allows access to the material.

**Mevis & Van Deursen**

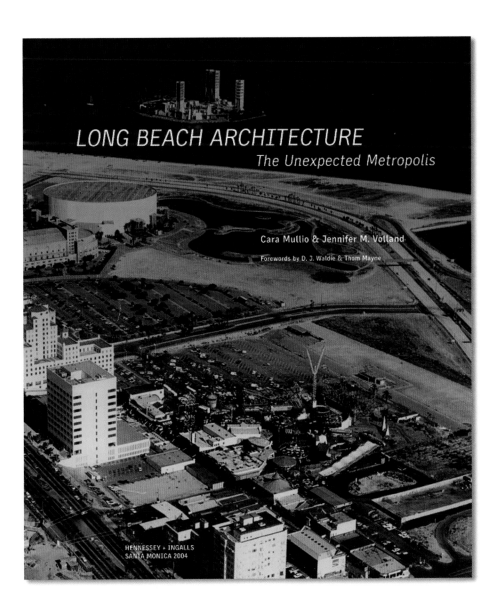

*Long Beach Architecture: The Unexpected Metropolis* incorporates an interesting and unusual use of color. Transparent color blocks are superimposed on black-and-white architectural imagery. Often, the blocks are subtle gradients of near-complementary colors. This use of color enlivens the industrial nature of the photography. True to the name of the book, the design offers an unexpected presentation of the urban landscape. **Michael Worthington**

# 6 Know That People See Color Differently

Color vision is a result of the way our eyes and brains interpret the complexities of reflected light. What we see is a result of different wavelengths of light stimulating parts of the brain's visual system. The three types of light receptors, called *cones*, are located in the retina of the eye and recognize these different wavelengths of light. Not every human being's receptors and interpretations of color are quite the same. In addition, some people have inherited genetic conditions, such as color blindness, that further affect color perception.

**Color Blindness Limits More Males**

Color blindness, of which several varieties exist, affects more males than females. People with monochromatic color blindness lack all cone receptors in their eyes and cannot see any color. People with dichromatic color blindness lack either red-green or blue-yellow receptors and cannot see hues in these respective ranges. People with color weakness, or anomalous trichromatism, can perceive a color but need greater intensity of the associated wavelength in order to see it normally. The natural aging process in humans may also reduce color vision and acuity.

Physical factors are one way that people see color differently. Another factor is technological. Color is read differently in print and on the screen. Pure RGB light appears different than reflected light (usually CMYK). Colors may also appear different because not every computer monitor and television screen is color-corrected and calibrated properly. Designers cannot be sure how their color choices are being experienced in these media.

**Color Alterations for Artistic Reasons**

Designers may alter color perception deliberately for artistic and semiotic reasons. They may choose to subjectively or artistically change what would be considered the accurate, normal, or natural color of things, and instead render it in a different color. When a color is the real and actual expected hue, it is called a local color. If it is unexpected or abnormal, it is referred to as occult color.

For example, a piece in which an apple is rendered in shades of blue would be an occult representation. A blue apple would cause the viewer to question why this familiar object is depicted in a strange and unnatural color and perhaps prompt deeper interaction with the design. This color alteration is essentially a creative interpretation or abstraction of the idea of seeing color.

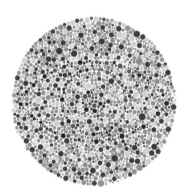

This simulation of a color blindness test graphic is like those used to diagnose red-green difficulties. People with this type of color vision deficiency cannot see the eye shape within the pattern. Several diagnostic tests are used in determining color blindness.

DCM (Doll Capital Management) sought to highlight the clear difference that makes its technology venture fund attractive to Asian investors. Bold graphics utilizing financial icons give an elegant simplicity to the presentation. Red was chosen as the dominant color because of its symbolic connection to luck in Asia. However, the similar tonal values in some of the monochromatic icon illustrations could be difficult for some vision-impaired people to fully appreciate.
**Gee + Chung Design**

## An Artistic Interpretation of Color

Dutch painter Vincent van Gogh (1853–1890) made a significant contribution to art through his astonishing use of color. Van Gogh used colors deliberately to capture mood and emotion rather than create realistic reproductions.

Technological advances in the chemistry of artists' pigments in the late 1800s, along with his own exposure to other Impressionists' work, freed van Gogh to use bright, intense color in his work. His palettes expanded, taking on the characteristics that made him famous.

Van Gogh painted rapidly, often using paint straight from the tube in thick impasto brushstrokes. His imaginative, vibrating, urgent color schemes changed the direction of art. He is one of the great fine art masters whose work can inspire designers.

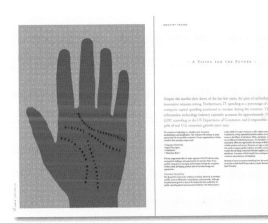

## Effective Color Contrast
### *Designing for People with Partial Sight and Color Deficiencies* by Aries Arditi, Ph.D

*Dr. Aries Arditi is Senior Fellow in Vision Science at Lighthouse |International. This information is based on his earlier work with |Kenneth Knoblauch, reprinted here by permission of the author.*

These are the three basic guidelines for making effective color choices that work for nearly everyone. Following the guidelines are explanations of the three perceptual attributes of color—hue, lightness, and saturation—as they are used by vision scientists.

**How does impaired vision affect color perception?**
Partial sight, aging, and congenital color deficits all produce changes in perception that reduce the visual effectiveness of certain color combinations. Two colors that contrast sharply to someone with normal vision may be far less distinguishable to someone with a visual disorder. It

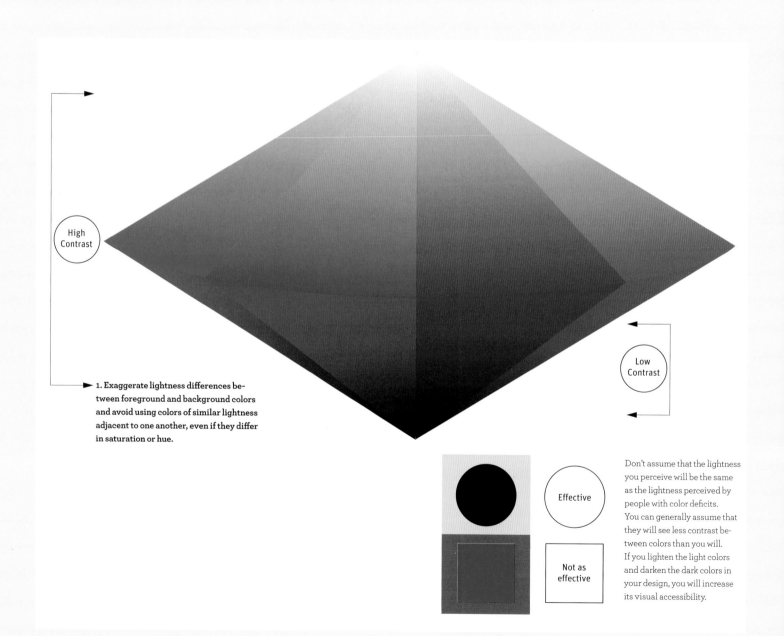

High Contrast

Low Contrast

**1. Exaggerate lightness differences between foreground and background colors and avoid using colors of similar lightness adjacent to one another, even if they differ in saturation or hue.**

Effective

Not as effective

Don't assume that the lightness you perceive will be the same as the lightness perceived by people with color deficits. You can generally assume that they will see less contrast between colors than you will. If you lighten the light colors and darken the dark colors in your design, you will increase its visual accessibility.

is important to appreciate that the contrast of colors, one against another, that makes them more or less discernible, rather than the individual colors themselves. Here are three simple rules for making effective color choices:

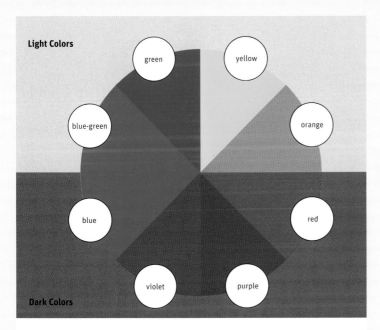

2. Choose dark colors with hues from the bottom half of this hue circle against light colors from the top half of the circle. Avoid contrasting light colors from the bottom half against dark colors from the top half. The orientation of this hue circle was chosen to illustrate this point.

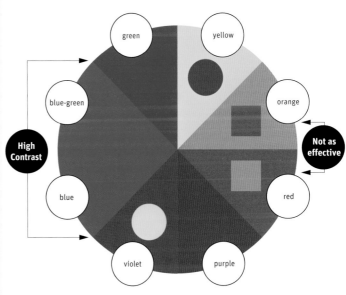

3. Avoid contrasting hues from adjacent parts of the hue circle, especially if the colors do not contrast sharply in lightness.

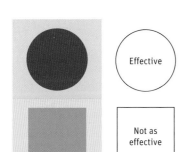

For most people with partial sight and/or congenital color deficiencies, the lightness values of colors in the bottom half of the hue circle tend to be reduced.

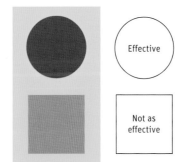

Color deficiencies associated with partial sight and congenital deficiencies make it difficult to discriminate between colors of similar hue.

"It is the contrast of colors, one against another, that makes them more or less discernible, rather than the individual colors themselves."
—Aries Arditi, Ph. D

Hue, lightness, and saturation, the three perceptual attributes of color, can be envisioned as a solid. (Please see page 13 for further explanation of these color attributes.)

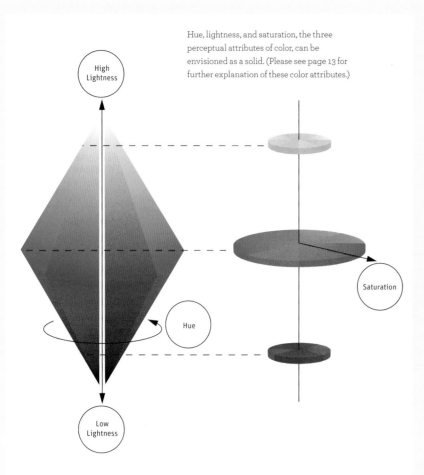

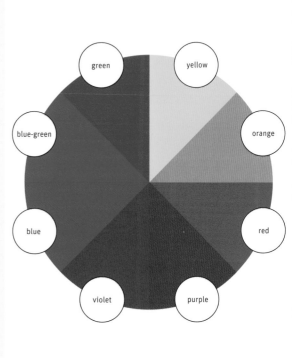

Hue varies around the solid; lightness varies from top to bottom; saturation is the distance from the center.

Hue is the perceptual attribute associated with elementary color names. Hue enables us to identify basic color categories such as blue, green, yellow, red, and purple. People with normal color vision report that hues follow a natural sequence based on their similarity to one another. With most color deficits, the ability to discriminate between colors on the basis of hue is diminished.

**About Lighthouse International**
Founded in 1905 and headquartered in New York, the nonprofit organization Lighthouse International is a leading worldwide resource on vision impairment and vision rehabilitation. Through its pioneering work in vision rehabilitation services, education, research, prevention, and advocacy, Lighthouse International enables people of all ages who are blind or partially sighted to lead independent and productive lives. The Arlene Gordon Research Institute of Lighthouse International works to expand knowledge in vision impairment and rehabilitation. Dr. Aries Arditi, a senior fellow for the Institute, has written several books and brochures of use to designers on computers, typography, color, and signage.

©1995–1997 The Lighthouse Inc. ©1999, 2002 Lighthouse International.

Lightness corresponds to how much light appears to be reflected from a colored surface in relation to nearby surfaces. Lightness, like hue, is a perceptual attribute that cannot be computed from physical measurements alone. It is the most important attribute in making contrast more effective. With color deficits, the ability to discriminate colors on the basis of lightness is reduced.

Saturation is the degree of color intensity associated with a color's perceptual difference from a white, black, or gray of equal lightness. Slate blue is an example of a desaturated color because it is similar to gray. A deep blue, even if it has the same lightness as slate blue, has greater saturation. Congenital and acquired color deficits typically make it difficult to discriminate between colors on the basis of saturation.

To a person with color-deficient partial sight, the left-hand panel might appear like the right-hand panel appears to a person with normal color vision. With color deficits, the ability to discriminate colors on the basis of all three attributes—hue, lightness, and saturation—is reduced. Designers can help compensate for these deficits by making colors differ more dramatically in all three attributes.

# 7   Assist in Mnemonic Value

*Yellow in London* eschews the traditional British national colors of red, white, and blue to mirror a foreigner's unconventional perspective on the city. It is memorable because it is unexpected.
**Usine de Boutons**

What designer doesn't want his or her work to be memorable to the audiences for which it was created? Color can be a powerful ally in that pursuit. Color can work as a mnemonic device itself, aiding people's memories. The word *mnemonic* comes from the Greek *mnemonikos*, which means "mind."

Many psychologists researching the process by which humans see and process visual information conclude that it is influenced highly by color. For example, the May 2002 *Journal of Experiential Psychology: Learning, Memory, and Cognition* reported the findings of one study that indicated that people did not remember falsely colored photographic scenes any better than those same scenes in black-and-white. They remembered the natural-colored images the best. Relating to psychology, when people think of a certain color, their minds form a corresponding color model; when they think pink, they actually visualize a rosy hue.

**Color Associations Aid Memory**
Different cultures have different associations with colors. Hues such as red and blue are not just colors; they are emotions, feelings, reflections, and memories. Seeing or thinking about

Color is memorable. Marketing research indicates that more than 80 percent of visual information is related to color.

color produces certain reactions in people. Color associations often become part of the semantic structure of color names themselves. For example, magenta, one of the first aniline dyes, was discovered shortly after the Battle of Magenta, which occurred near the northern Italian town of Magenta. The color was named for the battle and, therefore, indirectly for the town. Chartreuse is a yellow-green color named for the famous French liqueur of the same name. These types of associations are endless and can be leveraged to associate clients' products and services with colors.

### Color Symbolism
### Is Culturally Linked

Interestingly, the world seems divided into groups with similar ideas about color symbolism. In a 1999 study published by Kawade Shoboh Shinsha, a Japanese professor named Hideaki Chijiiwa grouped countries as follows: China, Taiwan, and Russia; Japan, Korea, and Finland; the Netherlands, Germany, Italy, the United States, Canada, New Zealand, Australia, and Singapore; France, Brazil, and Portugal; and India, Laos, and Bangladesh. Cultural factors are at work here, and understanding the similarities and differences in audiences will always

make for better design in our increasingly global community. (For a look at color associations, see the Color Index in Chapter 3.)

Cultural, political, and linguistic factors, including both abstract and symbolic components, affect our perception of colors. Color motivates a response because of memories. A person may buy the green-colored soap packaging because it reminds him or her of fresh-mown grass, for example. Couple visual information with the expected fragrance—green soap that actually smells like grass— and the design is even more effective.

### Proprietary Color

A further enhancement is the idea of developing a proprietary color that represents a client. Associating distinctive colors with products and services is one of the cornerstones of brand identity work. Some of the world's most memorable companies have strong connections to color— think of Kodak's chrome yellow and Fuji's bright green film boxes. Whether or not it is possible to trademark a color is an ongoing battle, generating many lawsuits, but color is an important branding tool.

Bart Crosby's design for the AIGA Chicago newsletter is linked to the no-nonsense, mid-western ethos of Chicago. This treatment is powerful and crisp, using black and white as proprietary colors. The same colors would be out of place for a newsletter in Los Angeles, San Diego, or Honolulu. Crosby's use of black and white printing is dynamic, using black boldly with sharp edges and scale change. The weight of the rule, matching the weight of the letter-forms, contrasts with the refined and detailed Bodoni serifs.
**Crosby Associates**

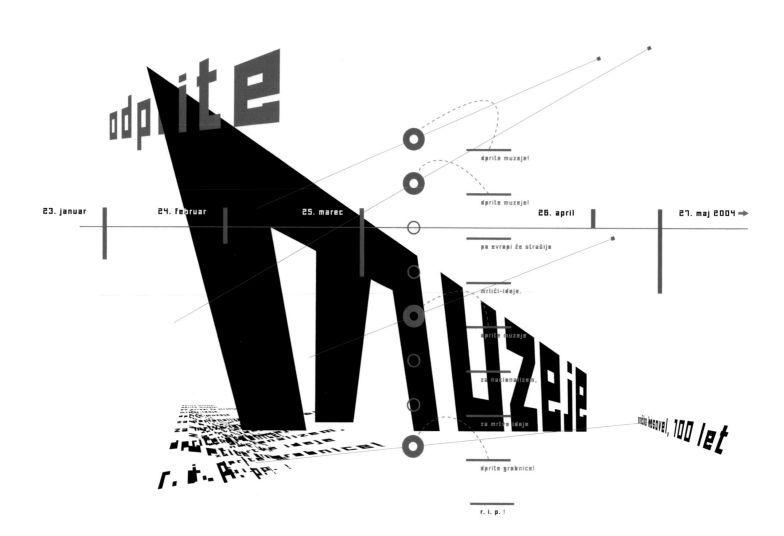

Designed by Edouard Cehovin, large black, white, and red graphics positioned on the walls of a parking garage assist motorists in locating their cars and enliven the traditionally dull environment. The different-colored shapes can be used effectively as mnemonic devices.
**Kontrapunkt**

**Color Temperature**

*We can identify a sensation of temperature when refer-*
*ring to colors—some are cool (greens, blues, violets) and*
*some are warm (yellows, oranges, and reds). There is a*
*contrary aspect to color temperature because color can*
*rarely be warm and cold at once.*

Warm colors are often associated with strong emotion
and heat, while cool colors are linked to calmness and the
refreshing chill of sky and sea. We feel color temperature—
red literally makes our pulse race, while blues slows
heart rates.

Considered specifically at the time of color selection,
variations on and utilization of color temperature can be
useful in causing designs to be more memorable and to
better serve the needs of clients and their customers.

**Cool Colors**

Here are examples of
designers working with
cool colors in interesting
ways. From a theater poster
in Stockholm to a contract
furnishings showroom
environmental design
to upscale dog toy packaging, cool shades of blues
and greens are the
unanimous choice.
**Above:**
Sweden Graphics
**Right:**
Carbone Smolan Agency
**Below:**
Concrete

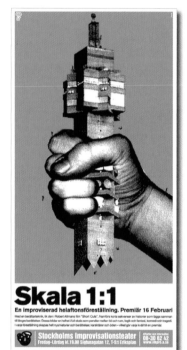

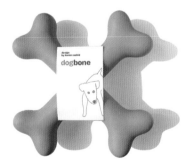

Saturation is the degree of color intensity associated with a color's perceptual difference from a white, black or gray of equal lightness. Slate blue is an example of a de-saturated color because it is similar to gray. A deep blue, even if it has the same lightness as slate blue, has greater saturation. Congenital and acquired color deficits make it difficult to discriminate between colors on the basis of saturation.

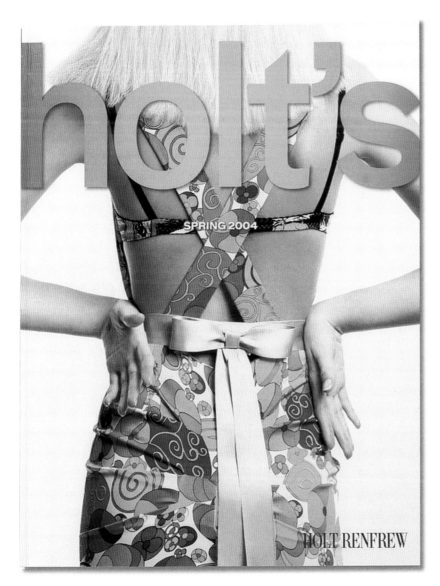

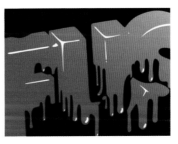

**Warm Colors**
Warm colors work to boost appeal in these projects, including bright earth tones for a specialty coffee store, gradient oranges for a department store catalog cover and melting red-orange for a television spot. Warm colors tend to advance, bringing the message to the viewer.
**Left:**
Concrete
**Right:**
Hunter Gatherer

# 8 Think About Composition

Artists have been pursuing the ideal standard for proportion and composition since ancient times. The classical Greeks established the Golden Mean, also called the Golden Section or Golden Proportion, as a mathematical ratio and unifying force. The Golden Mean is a standard proportion for width in relationship to height in which the division of a given unit of length equals the ratio of the longer part to the whole. So, if the longer part is called x, and the shorter part 1–x, then 1–x is to x as x is to 1.

The Greeks understood that a small part relates to the whole, both in life and art. Other creative scholars and practitioners employ their own methods. The selection and positioning of design elements, specifically the ratio of the individual parts to one another, is a matter of the designer's personal judgment. Balance, symmetry, hierarchy, space, repetition, and rhythm are all organizing principles to be considered and used. Unquestionably, color affects all of these principles.

Color can be used to make the eye travel, comfortably or not, and pick up information from a design. Transitions can be produced using line, shape, contours (edges of shapes), and motifs in various colors for both images and typographic elements in compositions. The repetition of elements and colors create a kind of rhythm, whether a smooth flow or a jerky visual movement, as dictated by the designer's choices. The echoing of colors is a kind of repetition that brings unity to a composition. Repetition does not require exact duplication of elements; similarity, or near likeness, works. Variations in hues and their specific placement create interest, while intervals of visual silence (e.g., a dark solid-color background) between repeating elements provide rest stops for the eye. Areas of pure white and pure black boost impact and contrast.

Some designers choose to disregard traditional ideas about proportion and balance in order to emphasize extremes of scale. This creates emphasis and communicates messages through exaggeration. Differences in the scale and proportion of a color can create a focal point in a design composition.

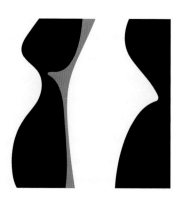
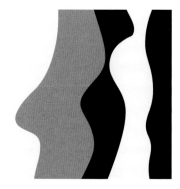
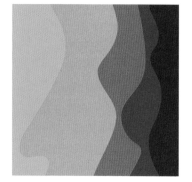
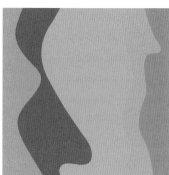

**Contour Color Study**
Whether few or many colors are used, variations in composition can dramatically change a design. The four squares shown here demonstrate different proportions of color usage. Note the vibrating contours and their effect on eye movement. Also visible is the effect of vibrating and vanishing boundaries between colors.

**Color can be used as a visual linking device
to build balanced and effective compositions.**

Equal proportions of the
complementary colors blue
and orange.

Hues of a double triad
(green, red-orange, violet)
used in equal proportions.

**Proportion and
Saturation Study**
Two pairs of color schemes—
one a pair of complements,
the other a triad—are shown
here in differing ratios.
Note how the ratio changes
impact how each color is
perceived and how these
shifts affect the mood of the
composition.

Proportions reassigned to
allow dominant (blue) and
subordinate (orange) areas.

Proportions reassigned to
allow dominant (green), subordinate (violet), and accent
(red-orange) areas.

Proportions and saturation
modified, full blue on top,
pure orange with a slightly
de-saturated blue in the
middle, and de-saturated
blue below.

Proportions and saturation
modified to display a lower
level of contrast.

FIDM (Fashion Institute of
Design & Merchandising)
Museum and Galleries, un-
der the creative direction of
Tamar Rosenthal, presented
the *Marimekko: Fabrics,*
*Fashion, Architecture*
exhibition to spotlight this
internationally renowned
design company. The event
was sponsored in part by
Crate & Barrel, which created in-store displays using
the exhibition poster. The
composition of poster and
environment reflect Ma-
rimekko's signature style.
**Vrontikis Design Office**

"All colors are the friends of their neighbors and the lovers of their opposites."—**Marc Chagall**

Freewheel is a mobile phone powered by a dedicated wi-fi network with over 1,000,000 hot-spots. Collins created the system, digital product language, and packaging for the brand. The energetic lines on the packaging express the idea of a free and strong wi-fi signal that is available almost everywhere. The exuberant color palettes express diversity, precision, and harmony. The white background creates the strong contrast and dynamic of the packaging. **Collins**

## The Principle of Figure and Ground

Figure and ground is an important principle in design. When we see relatively large plain elements as backgrounds to smaller, more distinct ones, we are experiencing *figure and ground*. This principle contradicts the assumption that smaller objects are always less significant—sometimes they dominate, especially due to color choice.

Compositions in which the figure and ground are not immediately distinguishable often seem lifeless. Elements that differ in color and value from the background draw the eye in first almost regardless of their hue. Light figures on a dark ground often seem more luminous, sometimes even mysterious—an effect exploited by Renaissance painters, for example.

The figure and ground principle, coupled with color theory ideas such as the observation that warm colors advance and cool colors recede, or that complementary colors provide rich contrast, allow a designer to create dynamic compositions.

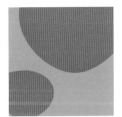

Symmetry is a distinct organizing principle in composition that can be further enhanced through the use of color.

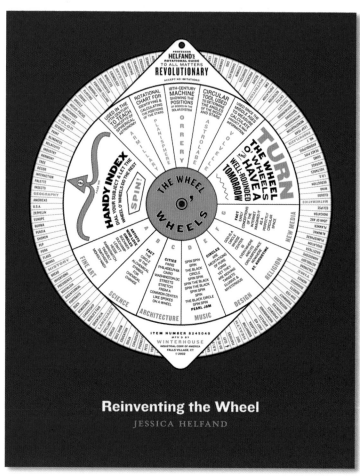

**Symmetrical Balance**
Symmetrical balance is achieved by mirroring often identical elements in a composition. Symmetry can be quite static, but this *Old York* poster, commemorating the 9/11 tragedy in New York City, achieves movement through the repeating shapes of the gradient orange clouds that surround the white focal point of the Twin Towers.
**Sweden Graphics**

**Radial Balance**
The *Reinventing the Wheel* book cover is a great example of radial balance. This is a composition balanced around a focal point. The designers created a *volvelle*, a calculation consisting of concentric circles, adapting an existing piece by retrofitting it with their own content. The complementary colors increase legibility.
**Winterhouse Editions**

**Closure or Visual Grouping**

Early twentieth-century German psychologist Max Wertheimer investigated how humans see form, pattern, or shape, in terms of group relationships rather than individual items. He discovered that proximity and size help objects relate visually. Closure, or visual grouping, is the ability humans have to unify incomplete patterns by bringing together the elements in their mind. The phenomenon occurs when a designer provides a minimum of clues, yet the viewer recognizes meaning in the pattern.

**Approximate Symmetry**

The poster for the film *Wolfsschlucht* demonstrates approximate symmetry, a composition in which elements that are not identical have the same apparent weight. The diagonal color blocks are not equal. The green, however, is balanced by the hue's complement in the form of a solid red figure on the right.
**Format Design**

**Asymmetry Balance**

The book cover for the definitive edition of William S. Burroughs' breakthrough novel *Junky* has a distinctive handmade quality. The composition features a hand-lettered title, a character illustration, and a hand-drawn version of the publisher's logo. The asymmetrical spots of yellow and orange leap from the neutral background.
**Powell**

# 9 Use Standardized Color Systems

Increasingly, designers work across several media, including print, online, broadcast, packaging, and environment. Care must be given to create consistent reproduction results in a variety of manufacturing processes and materials. Consistent colors are managed through the use of standardized color systems.

**Several Choices of System**

For inks on paper, designers use the PANTONE® Matching System, TOYO, ANPA, or DIC (Dai Nippon Ink Colors). In the United States, the most ubiquitous color formula specification system, especially for spot colors, is PANTONE®, with colors referred to as PMS and a series of numbers (e.g., PMS185 is a bright red). These standardized colors are offered in thousands of hues as well as specialty inks such as metallics, tints, and fluorescents. Standards for soy-based ink colors are also available. Most graphic software systems (especially Adobe products), computer monitors, and ink-jet printers include palettes and simulations that correspond to these standard color systems. However, it is critical that digital devices such as monitors be properly calibrated to correctly simulate colors.

Offset lithography is a four-color process whereby layers of cyan, magenta, yellow, and black (CMYK) are applied to paper surfaces in varying amounts via dot patterns. Larger presses often include additional units to accommodate spot colors and may even have coating units to apply finishes such as varnish and aqueous coating. Standardized process color guides, which show percentages for each of the CMYK values, are available in SWOP, a printing standard used in the United States and Asia, and EURO (for Euroscale), used in Europe.

Color systems offer specification guides in a variety of formats, including binders with tear-off chips and fan-style guides. These guides also show what the colors look like on coated and uncoated paper stocks. Some of the latest innovations in standardized color systems are in digital color matching. For example, PANTONE® has a guide that matches spot colors with their process color equivalents and the output from several digital press systems. Guides like this ensure that a client's logo on stationery matches that in ads and brochures.

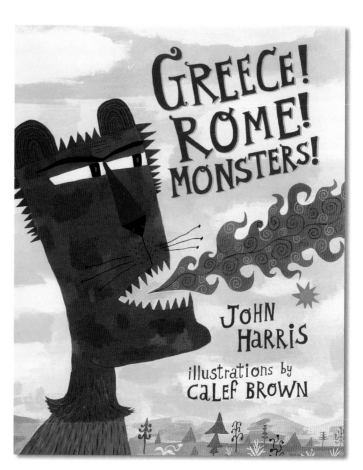

*Greece! Rome! Monsters!* is a children's book that introduces mythological stories in an innovative and engaging way. The challenge was to reproduce illustrator Calef Brown's vivid paintings in four-color process. Designer Jim Drobka incorporates hand-lettered typography that responds to the illustrations. The standardized color systems allowed for consistent color reproduction. **Getty Publications**

"We don't tend to think of paint chips as information infrastructure. Yet when everyone in the world is using the same ones, they become a communications protocol... It greases the wheels of big, fast global culture."
—J. C. Herz, *Wired*, "Living Color" October 2002

**Color Standardization Beyond Print**

Architects and environmental graphic designers also use a version of the PANTONE® system, as well as others, to specify textiles, paints, and plastics. Often, these must coordinate with printed components as well.

For color on screens, whether for online or broadcast, different color systems are used. To specify online colors, there are several guides for Web colors that correspond to print-based notation systems. However, graphics software, especially those for website creation, are equipped with Web-safe calibrations. For television, consistent color specification in the NTSC (in the United States) or PAL (in Europe and Asia) color space used by broadcasters is problematic. (See page 92 for further explanation of broadcast color.) The variance in preproduction, postproduction, and at-home viewing screens can be very different. There are no guides per se, but graphics software programs can convert standard CMYK colors into RGB, and good approximations of standard colors can be expected.

Color management is a complex technical issue. It is also an area that is constantly changing technologically. Designers must stay abreast of latest developments and consult with their suppliers as well as their software manufacturers' websites. They should also take advantage of the many resources and products offered by GretagMacbeth, one of the industry leaders in color management.

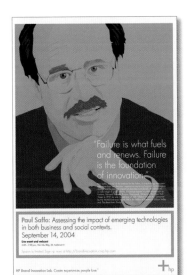

Posters for the HP Brand Innovation Lab's Speaker Series feature the speakers' photos rendered as monochromatic outline drawings set against a single field of one of HP's corporate colors. Spot colors like these can be consistently specified using standard color formulas. **SY Partners**

International Contract Furnishings sought to unify its collection of companies and thus established the ICF Group to provide a consolidated selling system. Marketing efforts include printer materials, advertising, online promotions, and retail stores, all designed for maximum brand coherence. That means there must be a consistent application of the corporate identity across a variety of reproduction processes and materials, as seen here.
**Carbone Smolan Agency**

"Color is my day-long obsession, joy, and torment."
—Claude Monet

These HUGA T-shirts are for sale through the designer's online store. Being able to consistently produce the same color over time is a concern for the company. Standardized specification and color formulas for silk-screening inks make this possible and can be guaranteed if the same silk-screen ink manufacturer is used for all products. Many designers use PANTONE® coated color chips when specifying color for silk-screening. **Hunter Gatherer**

## Color in Politics

Since the days of ancient Rome, competing political factions have used color to symbolize their group's ideologies. There are exceptions, from country to country, but the following standard associations of color and politics generally apply worldwide.

The Green Party is associated with environmentalism, and green is often used to represent Islamic parties. Blues typically represent conservative parties, except in the United States, where blue is associated with the more leftist Democratic Party. Red is historically associated with socialism or communism but now also represents the Republican Party in the United States. Both anarchism and fascism have used black, while white has been linked nearly universally to pacifism, most likely due to the white flag of surrender. Yellow is often used to represent libertarianism and liberalism. Other colors have been employed, but these are the enduring colors of politics.

The Radio Barcelona exhibition required design in several media. Standardized color systems were used to achieve consistency in items such as painted walls, printed materials, and silk-screened merchandise. Rich, deep blacks and geometric patterns in white and pale blue distinguish the design and give it a sense of both technology and mystery.

**BASE Design**

Pentagram's London office was engaged to develop a new identity and package design for PANTONE®. Designers John Rushworth (Partner-Graphics) and Daniel Weil (Partner-3D) and their teams positioned PANTONE® to consumers as the color authority that enables them to make color-sensitive decisions. The solution was to transform the chip icon into a swatch guide. This is a format that consumers typically understand from buying paint and wallpaper.

**Pentagram**

Instead of a single gallery guide for the American Tableaux exhibition, eight versions were produced, suggesting the plurality of interpretive possibilities contained in the theme. A new guide was available each month during the eight-month run of the show. **Walker Art Center**

# 10 Understand Limitations

It has been said that necessity is the mother of invention, and naturally, that applies to graphic design as well. Sometimes budget constraints are a limiting factor that wears down and frustrates designers. Stretching design dollars does not mean that down and dirty must be ugly and ineffective. Effective color usage can provide impact and beauty on a limited budget. Financial concerns are not the only reason for limiting the number of colors specified; sometimes it is a question of aesthetics as well.

Using only a few colors, perhaps on colored stocks, can result in a rich-looking piece. Pushing the boundaries with limited resources often means pushing the limits of production technology or thinking of new ways to incorporate old manufacturing techniques and materials. Stretching design dollars means embracing and leveraging limitations. However, it is best to understand the client's budget up front so designs can be formulated within it.

## Delivery Media Affects Color

There is a vast difference between the way color works on coated versus uncoated paper stocks. It is important to design and prepare artwork correctly for the paper type being used in order for the specified colors to look their best. Uncoated stocks absorb more ink, so color tends to sink or flatten unless separations are made to compensate for this. Halftone dots in color images tend to spread and deform on uncoated paper, a problem known as dot gain. Therefore, scanning and separations must compensate by opening the dots more so colors will appear to be at normal densities.

Coated stocks are made by casting the paper against highly polished, heated steel drums. The result is a harder surface that provides what is known as ink holdout, meaning that the color stays on the surface and is not absorbed into the paper. Both paper types have their own appeal, and colors will look great on each if the designs are properly prepared.

Miracle Creations is a designer toy shop in Singapore that sells interesting collectibles sourced from around the world and manufactures its own unique handmade toys as well.

The corporate identity incorporates magical and fairy tale creatures. Only Rhodamine Red (in positive and reverse color formats) was used, in order to limit costs. The red is fun and

stands out against the stark white, giving the piece a surreal essence due to the unnatural imagery color. **Kinetic**

"Design depends largely on constraints."
—Charles Eames

Color on screens—computer monitors or television sets—has its own limitations. A designer's biggest challenge is the inability to control the end product; each screen's calibrations and display properties are beyond the reach of standardized color specifications. For example, Macintosh and Windows operating systems use different platforms and protocols, and color can look very different in each.

Manufacturers work within a variety of technical parameters. Consumers can also make personal adjustments in image quality and color saturation. The result is that designers never really know whether their work is being viewed exactly as they intended it to or not.

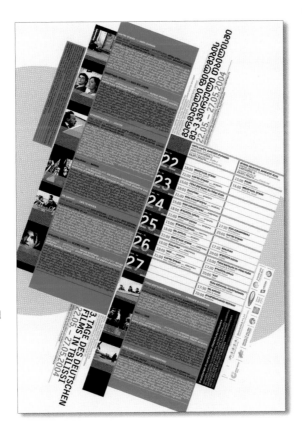

### Color on Paper

The key to great color on paper is working closely with your printer both in preproduction and on press.

- Tell your printer up front if you'll be specifying coated or uncoated paper stock.
- Get samples of the paper. Ask for "commercial printed samples" because these are actual print jobs from designers like you, and you can see real-world results. If your printer has run this stock before, ask for these samples as well.
- Provide your printer with any production and technical information you may have from the paper manufacturer. They often have great guidelines.
- As the printer to create separations for uncoated stocks, or colored paper.
- Let your printer know in advance if you'd like to use specialty inks such as soy based, metallic, or fluorescent.
- Request an "ink drawdown," which is a sample of the ink you've chosen on your actual paper stock.
- Add fluorescent ink touch plates under large areas of four-color process to add vibrancy to image color on uncoated papers.
- On press, make sure your printer takes both a wet and dry ink-density reading. Because uncoated stocks take longer to dry, the variances could be dramatic. Make sure the printer records this if there is a possibility of future reruns on the job.
- Preparation saves time, money, and disappointment and is the key to getting great color on paper.

This is the program for the *Tag Des Dutchmen Films in Tbilisi* film festival. It is printed with two colors on the back of the event poster. The program contains a schedule, film descriptions in two languages, and still images from each movie. Transparencies, pattern, and typography all work to produce a strong visual statement.
**Andrea Tinnes**

**How We Perceive Color over Time**

Aging is a natural human limitation. Color perceptions and preferences change with a person's age.

A study in Germany conducted by anthropologist Dr. Manuela Dittmar showed that age group differences in both males and females affected color preferences significantly. With advancing age, people's preference for blue steadily decreased, while the popularity of green and red increased.

The results suggest that color preferences can change over the course of the adult lifespan. These changes might be attributed to alterations in the ability to discriminate colors, the yellowing of the crystalline lens of the eye, and the decreased functionality of the retina's blue cones.

SamataMason was the Creative Director for this Appleton Paper promotion, consisting of a series of small books created by different designers and contained in a black case. Each book interprets the same theme and utilizes the same black and red color palette. The restrictions, only red and black, no imagery forced each designer to rely on content rather than style.

Sean Adams and Terry Stone wrote and designed a tongue-in-cheek "sociological" study of the design world. The restrictions allowed for a wide range of subjects and issues while creating a sense of unity. **AdamsMorioka**

"Make more from less."
—Sean Adams

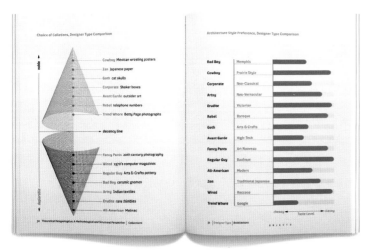

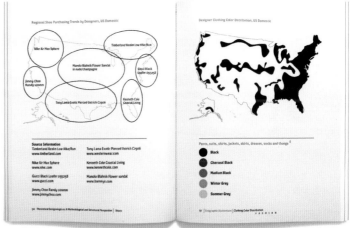

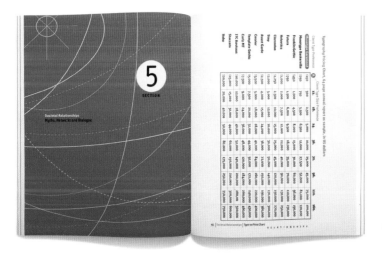

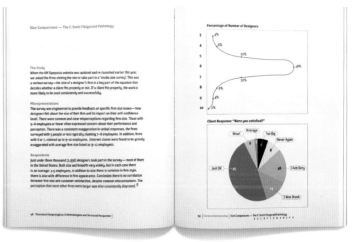

# Using color on screens should carry this warning: WYSIPNWYG (What You See Is Probably Not What You'll Get).

### Color On Screen: Design for Web & TV
by Victor Bornia

### Color and Web Design

Any use of color online—intended for viewing by the masses on personal computer screens—is far more of a hit-or-miss affair than color on paper. Once the design is online, it will be viewed on different platforms (Macintosh, Windows, etc.), each with their own gamma curves on different monitors (e.g., CRT, LCD), each set to brightness and contrast levels that no designer can control. That deep, lush burgundy you specified might be blown out to fire engine red, while that subtle pattern of darker hues you designed as a background may well end up a solid black. However, the disparities are not that ridiculous now that technology has advanced, and most people view websites in 24-bit color.

### Basic Web Design Tips

Test your design on both Macintosh and Windows computers. See the resulting variances for yourself. Try simulating a variety of brightness and contrast levels to see how your design stands up.

Understand graphics formats. The basic rule is that images composed of solid colors (type, icons, etc.) should use GIF; photos or complex images should use JPEG. Try both when exporting your graphics for the Web to see what works best— creating the smallest and best looking files.

### Color and Broadcast Design

The problem with designing for broadcast is similar to taking your design to the computer screen (which is RGB) and preparing it for print (to CMYK). However, rather than go flat or dull, colors now explode. This is because the standard television color space for video in the United States is NTSC (National Television System Committee). PAL (Phase Alteration by Line) and SECAM (*Systeme Electronique Couleur avec Memoire*), in Europe and Asia, all use a different gamma curve for luminance than your computer monitor.

What you see on your computer monitor will only get you so far in predicting what you will see on video. Only using an NTSC monitor allows you to see what the design will really look like. Most video graphics software (e.g., Adobe After Effects) have a built-in shortcut—a broadcast safe filter that attempts to automate making your colors ready for television.

### Basic Broadcast Design Tips

Always view your work on a properly calibrated NTSC monitor. If that is not possible, use a television with a video-in jack. It will serve as a NTSC monitor and will be more accurate than viewing on your computer monitor.

Do not trust built-in filters exclusively to go broadcast safe. Use your own eyes; sometimes de-saturating an image works best. At other times, adjustments to the brightness or contrast will be required.

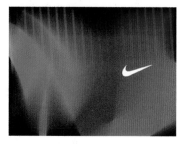
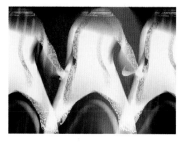

instant go

Motion Theory and Weiden + Kennedy/Tokyo collaborated to merge graffiti, an urban art form, and sophisticated motion graphics to promote Nike Presto to a Pan-Asian market. Colorful graffiti paintings literally come off the wall in animated television commercials. Graphics are intercut with Tokyo and Shanghai street scenes set to the music of Japanese DJ Uppercut, capturing the spirit of art, music, and culture of contemporary Asia.
**Wieden + Kennedy/Tokyo**
**Motion Theory**

**Chapter 5**
# Color Systems

A system is a set or arrangement of things that are related and form a unity or whole. A system is also an established way of doing something. With that in mind, we take a range of approaches in looking at color systems, including color forecasting, systems in art history, a view of how Sean Adams takes inspiration from objects in our environment to select color systems, and an examination of eleven projects by designers who practice in a variety of media.

# Thinking About Color Systems Trends and Forecasting

> "The forecasting business is notoriously intuitive. Forecasters work too far in advance of the market to offer the client any hard and fast data beyond their own track record."
> —Rick Poynor, *Obey The Giant*

Several companies, designers, and associations do market research on color to establish trends and predict changing cultural preferences that impact all areas of design. A variety of indicators, including consumer testing and surveys, help these color forecasters issue projections and define color palette preferences they believe will rise, fall, or maintain popularity. Most design-driven industries keep these projections in mind when developing their products.

Some industries find that color trends change rapidly; others are less subject to fluctuations in taste and style. The fashion industry is perhaps the most susceptible to trend. However, interior design, especially home furnishings, and automotive design are subject to fluctuations as well. Youth-oriented goods and services in every category feel the effects of shifting color trends.

The major U.S. forecasters are the PANTONE® Color Institute, the Color Association of America (CAUS—the oldest forecasting service in the country), and the Color Marketing Group (a nonprofit international association of 1,500 color designers). These groups provide forums, workshops, and reports on an annual and seasonal basis.

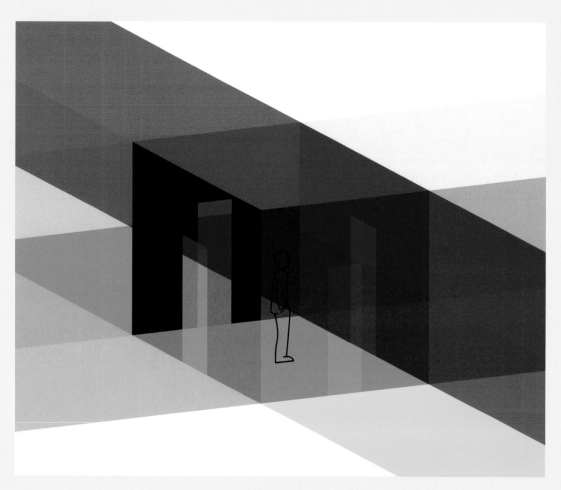

Color trends are huge design variables. Color forecasting helps designers look into the future to try to understand what colors will be not only fashionable but appropriate for their projects. One way to create work that has lasting appeal is to use the rainbow spectrum colors shown in this illustration for Quattroporte by Marco Morosini. **Marco Morosini**

## Color Forecasts:
## Where Do They Come From?
## By Leatrice Eiseman

From international runways to America's own designer collections, the march of models in the latest trend of colors will ultimately wend its way into and greatly influence the color of interior furnishings, automobiles, and all manner of consumer goods, including product packaging, advertising, websites, and point-of-purchase appeal.

The designers themselves are the stars of the show. They are attuned to and inspired by the hues they choose for a given season: they mold and manage color so that it attracts and stimulates the consumer's eye.

Obviously, fashion designers feel that color is an integral element of their work and recognize the emotional tug at the consumer level. The colors that appear first in fashion will trickle down inevitably to other design sensibilities, including graphic design.

In this modern age of instantaneous global communication, the pecking order is not as rigid as in the past, when new colors were first embraced by fashion, where they remained firmly entrenched for several seasons (or years) before designers and manufacturers adapted them for other design areas. Today the crossover of colors can happen within a matter of days as graphic designers access and adapt to the latest trends.

In the late 1980s, environmentalism was gaining ground as a sociological issue. That encouraged the use of recycled paper and discouraged the use of toxic chemical inks that were used in bolder colors. As a result, nonbleached hues such as beige and off-white became the colors of the moment in consumer goods, including clothing, home furnishings, packaging, and paper.

More recently, the graphic arts industry has spawned some of the most creative and unique color combinations and outrageous images that are constantly flashing on www.whatever.com. Colors bombard the public from a variety of other venues as well—from point-of-purchase to slick magazines, newspapers, catalogs, and billboards to the ubiquitous fashion reports on MTV, E! Entertainment Television, and CNN. As a result of all this exposure to color, the consumer is savvier than ever; he or she expects to see new color offerings in all products, so it behooves the smart designer to stay ahead of the curve.

To stay on the cutting edge of what is happening in color, it is imperative to understand the events that brought them to the forefront. From a purely psychological and sociological perspective, forecasted colors are inspired by lifestyle. For example, when designer coffee became the rage in the mid-1990s, coffee browns came forward in every area of design.

The attitudes and interests of the public at large—not only through entertainment and fashion icons—and their important social concerns, needs, desires, fears, and fantasies may spawn the newest color trends.

*Leatrice Eiseman, the executive director of the PANTONE Color Institute, is an internationally recognized color specialist. She is widely quoted in the media and is the author of several books, including PANTONE Guide to Communicating with Color. For more information, visit www.colorexpert.com.*

### Color Cycles

Many factors affect color trends, including:

· National cultural influences
· Music and entertainment; pop culture
· The economy (good or bad)
· World events (politics, wars, disasters)
· The shrinking global community
· Business and manufacturing demands
· Nature and environmentalism
· Shared technologies
· Nostalgia and futurism
· Psychological impact of certain colors

# Color Systems in Art and Design History

### Monet's Impressionism

Impressionism was a major art movement that emerged in France during the late nineteenth and twentieth centuries. Formed by a group of artists who shared related approaches and techniques, the hallmark of the style is the attempt to capture the subjective impression of light in a scene. Claude Monet is the archetypal Impressionist due to his devotion to the ideals of the movement. His famous studies *Haystacks*, *The Rouen Cathedral*, and *Waterlilies* record the subtle sensations of reflected light with the passage of time. His use of small brushstrokes of pure, intense, unmixed hues requires the participation of the viewer, whose eyes must mix colors and approximate the experience of natural sunlight.

The New York Public Library (detail)
**Sean Adams**

### Southwestern Adobe

The Southwestern Adobe style is based on the arts and crafts of the native peoples of the American Southwest, especially the Anasazi, Navajo, Apache, and Zuni Indians, and infused by Spanish and Mexican cultures. While the Southwestern style has been developing for centuries, it was popularized in the 1980s, almost to the point of cliché. Warm adobe sun-dried bricks used in house construction, textiles, baskets, and turquoise and silver jewelry all express and influence this style. Age-old materials of heavy rough-hewn wood, terra-cotta tile, and wrought iron against the landscape of the high desert with its expansive plateaus, distinctive mountains, and glorious red-orange sunsets can only be found in the Southwest.

Eat
**Pentagram**

### Mexican Folklorica

The timeless traditional Mexican folk arts and crafts combine traditions of Mesoamerican roots and inspirations with European, particularly Spanish, influences. The sacred and profane mix is a kind of Mexican baroque that incorporates native Indian decorative motifs, Catholic religious iconography, and lively narratives from everyday life. The bright, vivid colors are essential to the bold imagery, full of joy and human activity. The art and handicrafts are primarily of a representational figurative style, not at all abstract, and full of a simple splendor reflecting the character and ingenuity of Mexican artisans. There is a fluid romantic beauty and soulful rustic antiquity to this sun-drenched style.

Frida Diego (detail)
**Steff Geissbühler**

### African *Kente*

African art fuses visual aesthetics and imagery with spiritual beliefs and social purpose. Technical and artistic perfection merge in the gorgeous traditional *kente* cloth, which dates to twelfth-century Ghana. These textiles were originally worn by royalty and important figures of state for ceremonial occasions. Today *kente* cloth is often worn with pride as homage to African heritage. *Kente* comes from the word *kenten* ("basket") due to its resemblance to intricate basket designs. Skilled artists work to create balance and symmetry in the carefully woven designs. Each complex pattern of vibrant colors has deep symbolic meaning that represents the history, philosophy, ethics, and moral values in African culture.

24/7 (detail)
**Ph.D**

# Color Systems in Art and Design History

### Medieval Stained Glass

During the Gothic age, with its apex in the fifteenth century, the great cathedrals of Europe were built with spectacular pictorial stained glass windows. These luminous walls of glass were meant to lift men's souls closer to God. Stained glass is a bit of a misnomer, because most consists of colored pieces of glass held together with strips of lead. These transparent mosaics portray biblical history and church dogma. In the hands of medieval glaziers, the glass took on a jewel-like quality with the prevailing colors being red, blue, green, purple, purplish red, yellow, reddish yellow, and small amounts of white. Stained glass is one of the most beautiful forms of medieval artistic expression.

NEA Jazz Masters (detail)
**Chermayeff & Geismar, Inc.**

### Japanese *Ukiyo-e*

An art form both populist and sophisticated, *ukiyo-e* is the exquisite wood-block printmaking of the Edo period (1600s–1867) in Japan. *Ukiyo* translates as "floating world," an ironic wordplay on the Buddhist term for the sorrowful earthly plane. *Ukiyo* was the name given to the lifestyle of the urban centers involving fashion, the high life, and the pleasures of the flesh. *Ukiyo-e* images document both historical themes and popular culture, with an emphasis on kabuki actors, geishas, and landscapes. Early prints are spare and monochromatic. Later works are multicolored *nishiki-e* (brocade pictures) with a rich palette. These prints heavily influenced European artists, particularly French Impressionists.

*View From Here* (detail)
**Green Dragon Office**

### de Stijl

An art movement of the early 1920s, *de Stijl* (Dutch for "the Style") advocated simplicity and pure abstraction. De Stijl artists were interested in creating a universal style, accessible to all. Their utopian philosophical approach, advocating a purification of art and austerity of expression, was demonstrated in a variety of art forms as well as a journal bearing the name of the movement. Their carefully orchestrated straight lines and flat planes were a kind of ordering of reality. The color palette of primaries and achromatic colors (white, gray, black) produced abstraction. Although their output was small, de Stijl artists heavily influenced many subsequent design styles.

Museum Post und Kommunication (detail)
**Pentagram**

### Tropical Art Deco/
### Streamline Moderne

This style is best exemplified by the Miami Beach, Florida, oceanside district of small hotels, private residences, and commercial buildings developed in the 1930s and early 1940s. Tropical Art Deco, a later phase of Art Deco, is sometimes referred to as Streamline Moderne. This distinctive style incorporates clean modern lines and machine-inspired architectural forms of optimistic futurism mixed with local tropical imagery in the form of relief ornamentation of whimsical flora and fauna. Most remarkable is how delightfully the pale pastel color palette stands out in the bright sunlight reflecting off white sand beaches and sparkling waters.

Big Lawn Films (detail)
**Ph.D**

# Inspirations

Interesting color schemes can be motivated by everyday objects, the natural landscape, even wallpaper. Look beyond the object or place. Look at the colors.

## Moroccan Tile

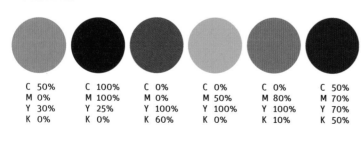

| C 50% | C 100% | C 0% | C 0% | C 0% | C 50% |
| M 0% | M 100% | M 0% | M 50% | M 80% | M 70% |
| Y 30% | Y 25% | Y 100% | Y 100% | Y 100% | Y 70% |
| K 0% | K 0% | K 60% | K 0% | K 10% | K 50% |

## Vintage Snapshots

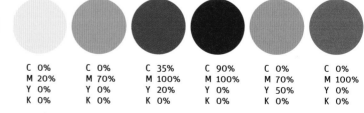

| C 0% | C 0% | C 35% | C 90% | C 0% | C 0% |
| M 20% | M 70% | M 100% | M 100% | M 70% | M 100% |
| Y 0% | Y 0% | Y 20% | Y 0% | Y 50% | Y 0% |
| K 0% | K 0% | K 0% | K 0% | K 0% | K 0% |

## Hawaiian Landscapes

| C 50% | C 60% | C 50% | C 20% | C 0% | C 10% |
| M 20% | M 30% | M 40% | M 25% | M 0% | M 0% |
| Y 0% | Y 30% | Y 100% | Y 40% | Y 0% | Y 0% |
| K 0% | K 0% | K 0% | K 0% | K 90% | K 0% |

## Wallpaper

| C 40% | C 60% | C 60% | C 0% | C 0% | C 0% |
| M 0% | M 30% | M 0% | M 30% | M 0% | M 15% |
| Y 25% | Y 0% | Y 60% | Y 75% | Y 0% | Y 15% |
| K 0% | K 0% | K 0% | K 0% | K 100% | K 0% |

Design Firm:

# Chase Design Group

Polly Pocket! Licensed Product Style Guides Design
Client: Mattel, Inc.

Polly Pocket! is a product line centered around a small toy doll. The first job assigned to Chase Design Group was to update the personality at the heart of the brand: Polly herself. This included exploring Polly's likes and dislikes, defining her style preferences, and giving her a lifestyle and friends. Next, an entire line of graphics, patterns, and illustrations was designed, along with concepts for soft and hard line products such as apparel, electronics, and activities that would support the brand.

The goal of these licensing guides is to create a line of products that parents and their four- to eight-year-old girls will want to buy and wear. Unlike many licensing brands, Mattel's brands are built on familiar toys but are not supported by entertainment properties such as movies and television shows. Therefore, the designs themselves must work hard to make a strong fashion statement that will appeal to consumers. Chase Design Group not only created the binders, but also designed the colorful graphics to be used to create the merchandise.

style guide | fall-winter 2004

contents

fall-winter 2004

The original Polly Pocket! illustrations lacked style and personality, so they were redrawn in a more modern, slightly anime style. The existing color palette was adjusted and expanded to be more fashion-forward and work better for apparel. A simple iconic style was developed for the art, pattern, and graphics so it can be maintained consistently throughout the product lines yet updated with seasonal

Produced twice a year, these guides feature predominantly lime green and red. This core palette was expanded to include orange and purple and allows for additions of seasonal colors as well.

Design Firm:

# Durfee Regn Sandhaus

*Only Skin Deep: Changing Visions of the American Self* Exhibition Design
Curators: Coco Fusco and Brian Wallis
Client: International Center for Photography

*Only Skin Deep* challenges some of the central myths and contemporary assumptions about American identity by showing how fluctuating conceptions of race and nation have been fixed or transformed through photographic strategies.

For this exhibition, DRS understood that the primary operative quality of the exhibition was "re-seeing." For example, re-seeing historical relationships we may have taken for granted, re-seeing moral structures associated with various images. The labels encouraged the viewer to see beyond pre-conceived or expected understandings by emphasis on new meanings suggested by titles, rather than on the more conventional emphasis of the artist.

"Pods" were specially fabricated to create spaces that would help organize the work and create more intimate viewing experiences for videos and allow for the display of small objects.

1999
Vanessa Beecroft (b. 1969)

VB 39, US NAVY SEALS, MUSEUM OF CONTEMPORARY ART, SAN DIEGO, 1999

Chromogenic print
COLLECTION OF ALBERTO CHEHEBAR, FLORIDA

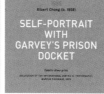

1995
Albert Chong (b. 1958)

SELF-PORTRAIT WITH GARVEY'S PRISON DOCKET

Gelatin silver print
COLLECTION OF THE INTERNATIONAL CENTER OF PHOTOGRAPHY, MUSEUM PURCHASE, 1995

ca. 1920
Baker Studio
Ray Jerome Baker (1880–1972)

A HAOLE HULA GIRL (ROSE HEATHER), HAWAII. HAOLE IS A HAWAIIAN WORD FOR ANY NON-HAWAIIAN FOREIGNER, ALTHOUGH MOST OFTEN USED FOR CAUCASIANS OF EUROPEAN DESCENT.

Real photo postcard
BISHOP MUSEUM, HONOLULU, HAWAII

1992
Charlene Teters (b. 1952)

MOUND TO THE HEROES

Digital-photo tapestry
COURTESY OF THE ARTIST

1946
Unidentified photographer

ATOMIC CLOUD DURING BAKER DAY BLAST AT BIKINI

Modern gelatin silver print
COURTESY NATIONAL ARCHIVES AND RECORDS ADMINISTRATION, COLLEGE PARK, MARYLAND

The transluscent panels in soft shades of yellow challenge the viewer to see or not see what is behind.

Panels and continuous table-height surfaces flow through the gallery, unifying the diverse elements and their display conditions. The subtle tones of the exhibition's design reinforces the concept of "re-seeing" beyond the blatant or obvious content of an image.

Design Firm:

# Hello Design

"Culture Shock Week" Website Interface Design
Client: The National Geographic Channel

The National Geographic Channel sought to promote its special week-long programming event called "Culture Shock Week" to drive television tune-in and attract new viewers to the channel. To help promote the on-air programming, an online photography contest was developed. Users submitted their own photos from around the world, revealing both foreign cultures and diversity within the United States.

"Culture Shock Week" unveiled taboos throughout the world by looking at forbidden rites and rituals in many cultures. An online identity and visual system was created to present this unique programming in a compelling user experience. The website featured an easy-to-use interface that was templated for reuse with the "Culture Shock Week" photo gallery and future promotional sites for the client.

The dominant color used is a rich dark red/maroon, chosen because it is earthy, bold, and vibrant. It resonates with the event's focus on culture, ethnology, and society. The boldness of the maroon grabs attention without being overwhelming, especially as it is balanced by black bars and the photos themselves.

A simple, scrollable interface allows users to browse additional information and images in a visual way, customizing the experience to the user. Program listings and descriptions about other "Culture Shock Week" shows are provided in an area of white type on a black background. Users can quickly seek additional information on the shows and support viewership of the channel.

The navigational system for the photo gallery appears as a series of vertical bars below the photo box. Thumbnail views that enlarge when selected allow users to browse as well as look at an image up close. This design encourages interaction with gallery content.

The site is bold and visually stimulating, with rich beautiful *National Geographic* photography that underscores the fascinating cultures, peoples, and rituals everywhere.

**Design Firm:**

# Liska & Associates

**2002 Product Catalog and Dealer Toolkit**
**Klein Bicycles**

Klein Bicycles is a favorite of professional racers and hardcore mountain bikers, but few outside that small circle of devotees knew of the brand's existence until recently. Since 2000, Liska & Associates has helped build the Klein brand and raise awareness in an audience that purchases luxury sports equipment.

These goals are accomplished by focusing on the proprietary advantages built into a Klein bicycle's design and by positioning Klein as a best-of-class brand. Two pieces that have been key to the successful brand efforts are the catalog and the dealer toolkit. Both heavily emphasize Klein's custom paint color program options.

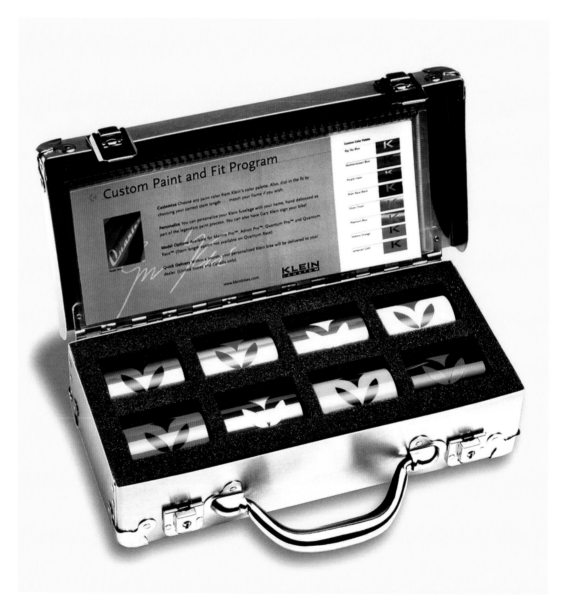

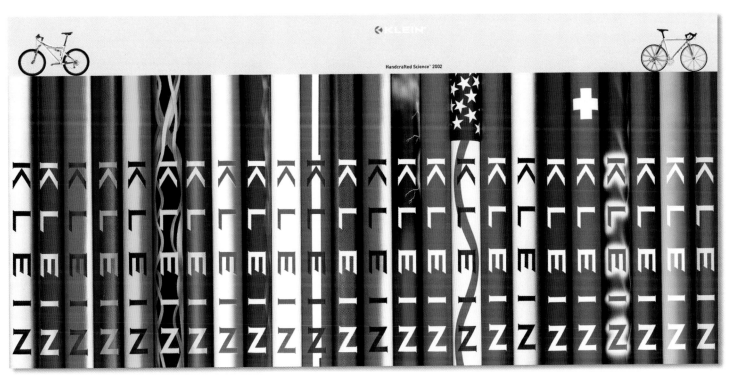

The Custom Paint Program Dealer Toolkit is a metal case of finish samples that dealers can use to demonstrate options to their customers. The painted samples give customers a much truer idea of the richness and depth of the bike colors than a printed swatch book could.

The Klein Catalog cover features the fourteen custom colors and ten international flag colors available on the bikes. Color is used to convey brand benefits by illustrating the many color choices available in a variety of Klein products.

**Design Firm:**

# Mevis & Van Deursen

*Los Amorales* by Carlos Amorales
Client: Artimo

*Los Amorales* is a book about a coherent series of works by the Mexican artist Carlos Amorales. The book was commissioned by the publisher Artimo and edited by Mevis & Van Deursen in collaboration with the artist. It chronicles an art project in a series of snapshot-like images and large, raw typography.

Amorales, working with professional fighters, organized Mexican wrestling matches in museums and art institutions. The wrestlers normally dressed like comic book heroes, but Amorales had them wear suits and masks based on a portrait of the artist. The book documents the behind-the-scenes story of meeting the wrestlers, creating the masks, and finally staging the wrestling matches.

The brutality of the typography, and green and red color, refer to authentic street posters that typically announce Mexican wrestling matches.

Captions appear large on the pages of the book, making them manifest and adding to the impact. The book was printed in partly with four-color process and partly with spot

color to keep costs down. However, the use of color became a deliberate way to mark the sections of the book and keep the Mexican wrestling vernacular.

Design Firm:

# Jessica Hische

**The Circle by Dave Eggars**
**Client: Vintage Books**

Jessic Hische's book cover for Dave Eggar's novel, The Circle, used the geometry of the circle and intersecting lines to communicate the complexity and maze of the tech world. The red and black offer a tone of danger and intensity. In a marketplace filled with books about the tech world, primarily in steely silver and blue, Hische's warm tones jump off the shelf.

As Hische explaons, "After working with Dave Eggers on *Hologram for the King* I was pumped to be brought on board to design his new book, *The Circle*. It was especially fun to design this cover, as I've spent the last two years living in San Francisco surrounded by the tech industry (my husband works for Facebook) and the story is set in an influential social media company. I also had to design a logo for the fictitious company, The Circle, and was inspired by the interweaving connectivity of social media sites and also knots that, once tight, are difficult to untie."

**Design Firm:**

# Vanderbyl Design

**Phonebooths and Mailboxes**
**Client: Teknion**

Michael Vanderbyl's publication, *Phonebooths and Mailboxes,* for the high-end furniture company, Teknion, is a dialogue about new technologies. The name "Phonebooths and Mailboxes," was chosen because both were once a common element in the urban landscape. Both are now becoming obsolete or redundant due to the ubiquity of mobile phones, digital transfer software, and e-mail—superseded by new technology.

The goal of *Phonebooths and Mailboxes* is to help organizations create an engaging and adaptable workplace, one that fosters a lively, collegial culture, with a greater level of creativity and innovation.

Vanderbyl approaches color from a surprising direction. Rather than opting for high contrast and bold color, Vanderbyl uses subtle tones of white, green, beige, and cream. The power here, is from the relentless commitment to this radical and aesthetically beautiful palette. The colors talk about the disappearance of older technologies and reinforce Teknion's commitment to quality and excellence.

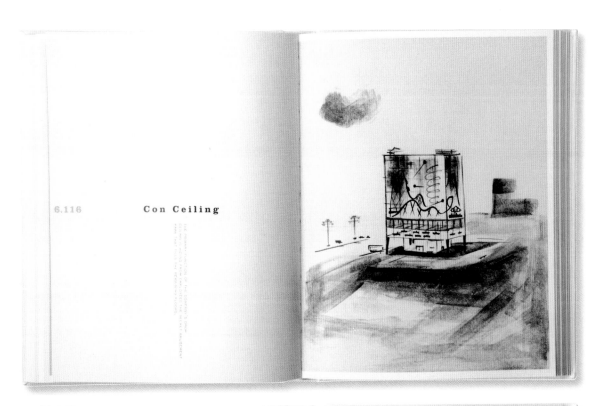

6.116    Con Ceiling

The lightest shades of green and beige are challenging. The obvious choice would be to use large black type to be legible. Vanderbyl does the opposite, using white large letterforms and delicate, small typography. The result, however, remains legible and clear.

Motion

**Design Firm:**

# Lippincott

**Hyatt Place**
**Client: Global Hyatt Corporation**

Service hotels are often clean, functional and efficient but remove the logo and you'd be forgiven for forgetting where you were staying. When Global Hyatt Corporation acquired the Amerisuites chain, they had the opportunity to bring Hyatt's unique brand story and values to the category. The newly-acquired chain was comparably under-invested, with a low room rate and a consistently drab presentation.

The new offering needed to sustain or increase occupancy at a slightly higher room rate, and attract the Gen-X road-warrior without losing the existing customer base.

Lippincott's challenge was to bring value and vitality to the chain. The name, Hyatt Place, and a visual identity are based on the idea of a gathering place. The bright colored geometric circles come together to form a sense of place or locality. The vibrant dots also form the letter "H". Lippincott used bold colors to design a concept that would resonate with guests on an emotional level and deliver moments of delight in their interactions with the brand.

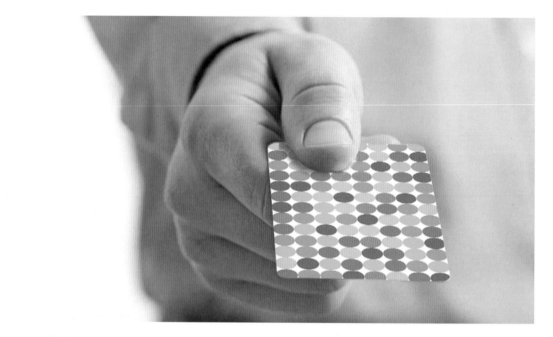

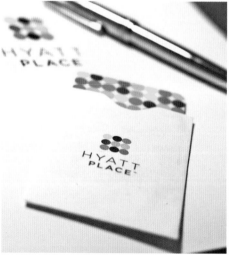

The color palette is based on clear and pure colors, typically used on white. The colors stop short of garish with slightly softer tones. This helps communicate vitality and home without feeling frenetic or circus-like.

Design Firm:

# Stripe

*Googie Redux: Ultramodern Roadside Architecture*, by Alan Hess
Client: Chronicle Books

The project tasked for Jon Sueda and Gail Swanlunc of Stripe was to redesign the book *Googie: Fifties Coffee Shop Architecture,* originally published in 1985. The redesign moves the book away from a pop culture souvenir book by treating the material as an architectural treatise. *Googie Redux* features the unconventional architecture of coffee shops and drive-in diners located primarily in Los Angeles in the 1950s.

The exaggerated forms of Googie structures were created to grab the attention of motorists. Each neon sign, angular glass, and thematic structure acted as a huge advertisement for the establishment it represented.

The design of the book embraced the idea of experiencing the architecture from a moving car. The extreme scale used on the typographic openers, the mortised shapes of the photographs, and the layout grid all mimic the Googie aesthetic.

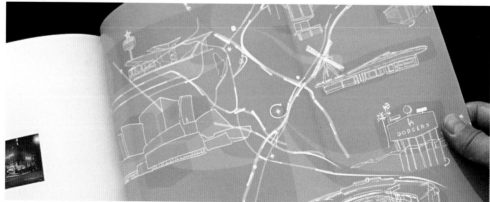

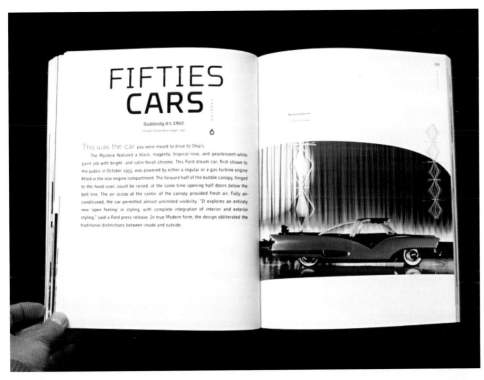

Large display typography, photo shapes, and a variety of graphic icons used throughout the book mimic a Googie itself.

The dominant color themes in the book include a range of sun-bleached Formica colors inspired by the images of the Googie diners. Color was used pragmatically to differentiate the sections of the book. Fields of color often underlie blocks of text, enlivening black-and-white spreads, as seen at right.

The more than twenty typefaces used in *Googie Redux* represent the diversity of typographic forms in the urban landscape.

Old photographs provide the majority of the color in the book. Taking cues from these images, the design utilizes pale blue and gold as accents.

**Design Firm:**

# Andrea Tinnes

Burg
Client: Burg Giebichenstein University of
Art and Design Halle

This vibrant set of cards announced the new visual identity of Burg Giebichenstein University of Art and Design Halle. The cards display the main elements of the new identity, encouraging the school's community to work and play with the identity.

The essence of the dynamic visual identity is to create differentiation between the high recognition and visibility of the BURG as an institution and the individual art and design personalities. This is achieved by a modular system composed of permanent and changing elements that can be combined in a playful way: the Burg logo and the university's name, the Burg letters, the custom typefaces Burg Grotesk, Burg Symbols and Minion, and a broad range of proprietary colors and atmospheric photos

*Concept and design: Andrea Tinnes, Wolfgang Hückel, Wolfgang Schwärzler, Anja Kaiser*

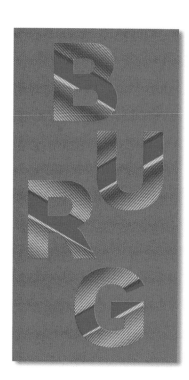

**Design Firm:**

# Shiffman Kohnke

*Frank O. Gehry: Flowing in All Directions*
**Client: Museum of Contemporary Art,
Los Angeles**

The book, *Frank O. Gehry: Flowing in All Directions*, for the Museum of Contemporary Art, Los Angeles, is the first book that looks at internationally famed architect Frank Gehry as an artist. This intimate portrait of Gehry's creative process reveals the details not only of how he works, but also of his total staff and office environment.

Tracey Shiffman's design presents the individuals and work in a direct and objective way. The color in the book exists primarily in the background of the images, or as a textural element. Pale yellow is used on sketch pages alluding to an architect's vellum paper. The rich diversity of the materials and forms of Gehry's work provides the visual power.

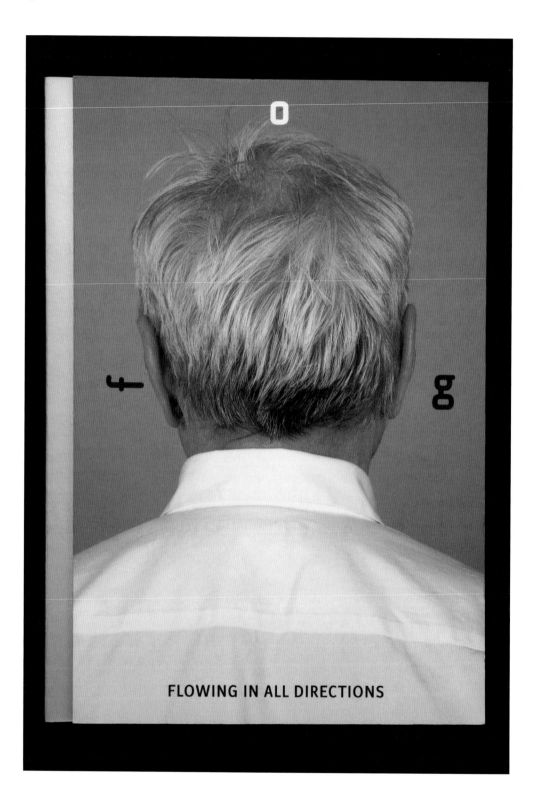

**Chapter 6**

# Color Talk

Many designers have difficulty articulating the rationale behind their color systems. At times, this is a result of having chosen a particular palette out of instinct. Choices made intuitively are hard to verbalize. In other instances, language for discussing the subtleties of tints and shades of hues and various color interactions simply escapes them. Nevertheless, talking about color with clients remains an important part of the design process.

"If one says "red" (the name of the color) and there are fifty people listening, it can be expected that there will be fifty reds in their minds. And one can be sure that all these reds will be very different."
— Josef Albers

# Talking About Color in Design

Talking about color will always be a challenge. Colors are associated with emotional states, symbolism, cultural meanings, and aesthetic preferences—all of which are deeply personal and experientially specific to the viewer. In addition, color terms do vary from culture to culture but also the language itself constantly evolves. For example, a language may start out with one or two names for blue and develop hundreds of names to describe ever more specific variations on the hue blue.

## Associations Help Determine Color Names

Color names are linguistic labels that humans attach to hues. Hues are determined by the physics of light reflection. The most dominant wavelength that is apparent is what gets named. Despite the complex systems that determine a color, most colors are named by association—either relative position on the color wheel, as in blue-green, or by reference to some natural object of that hue, such as the gemstone turquoise. Both terms can be used to describe the same hue. Changes in saturation can be ex-

pressed by adding a modifying label to the name, as in vivid turquoise. To describe changes in value, we generally add a reference to intensity, as in light turquoise or dark blue-green.

Special kinds of reflection provide additional modification, like metallic turquoise, sparkling blue green, and opalescent aqua.

Use of standardized color systems provides nomenclature for colors, as in the PANTONE® PMS names or Munsell's alphanumeric lexicon. However valuable and important it is to refer to colors in this manner during production, it is of little use in describing colors in conversations with clients. With all these variations in the language of color, the designer's best strategy for talking about color is simply to show it. Showing the entire proposed color system by applying it to various types of materials illustrates how the colors interact and provides confirmation that the designer has thought through color systematically. The choice of color seems less arbitrary and therefore is more likely to meet with client approval.

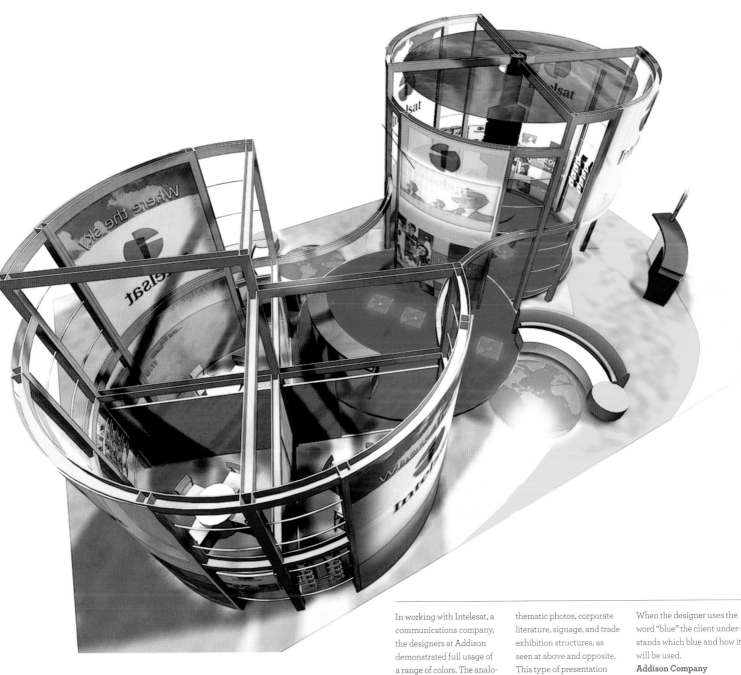

In working with Intelesat, a communications company, the designers at Addison demonstrated full usage of a range of colors. The analogous color scheme of blues, teals, and greens is shown in thematic photos, corporate literature, signage, and trade exhibition structures, as seen at above and opposite. This type of presentation allows designers to speak of color in a cohesive manner.

When the designer uses the word "blue" the client understands which blue and how it will be used.
**Addison Company**

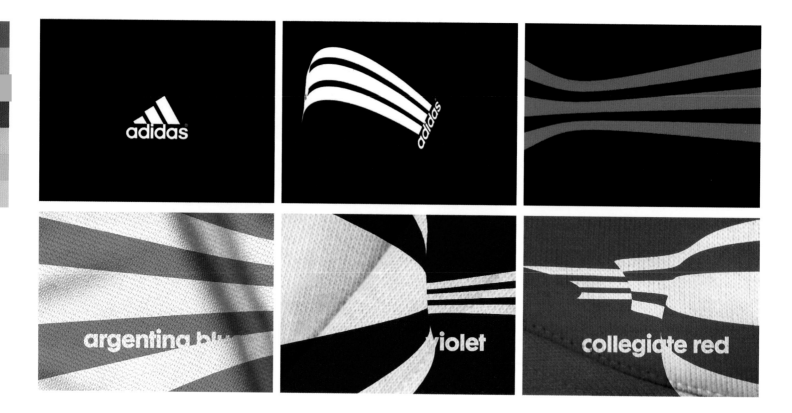

## Presenting Color to Clients

Set the tone for a great working relationship with clients in terms of color. We recommend the following tips to help get your color choices approved:

### Get Input Up Front

Survey your client about color when you start a project. Ask if they have ideas about color usage. Make sure you understand why they may or may not be tied to these preferences.

Get the client's corporate identity colors in CMYK, RGB, and spot color values to avoid guesswork.

### Please Yourself

Keeping in mind a client's objectives and input, concentrate on designing to your own high standards and selecting the colors that work best within given parameters.

Creativity, and especially color usage, is subjective. However, do develop a rationale for why you have selected a particular palette.

### Limit Choices

Present only your favorite color solutions and an alternative. Too many creative choices are confusing and convey the impression that you are indecisive.

### Control the Presentation

Show the color scheme in a variety of applications. If required, show color in print and on the screen. Seeing color in action makes it clearer and easier for a client to approve.

**Summarize the client's input and objectives. Explain why these colors, along with the other design elements, meet the project objectives and are the best choice.**

Involve the client in a discussion about color only relative to their objectives. Challenge revisions that will not meet the objectives effectively; accept changes that will.

In both the television spot for Adidas, above, color is an integral part of the concept of the piece. The spots show the new color palette for the products in an interesting yet simple approach. Since Adidas owns the three stripes that are part of its logo, the designers take advantage of the equity by bringing them to life and using them to guide the viewer through the swatch palette. **Brand New School, Adidas**

## Color Names

What's in a name? Searching for a way to describe that specific color in your layout? Here are some suggestions for descriptive color names:

| Reds | Yellows | Blues | Oranges | Greens | Purples | Blacks | Whites | Grays |
|---|---|---|---|---|---|---|---|---|
| Alizarin | Amber | Aqua | Apricot | Avocado | Amethyst | Anthracite | Alabaster | Ash |
| Berry | Banana | Azure | Carrot | Cactus | Aubergine | Carbon | Antique white | Chrome |
| Blood | Butter | Blueberry | Citrus | Celadon | Blackberry | Ebony | Coconut | Fawn |
| Brick | Cheddar | Cadet | Copper | Celery | Eggplant | Jet | Cream | Mist |
| Burgundy | Cornsilk | Cerulean | Coral | Chartreuse | Fuchsia | Lamp black | Ecru | Nickel |
| Cadmium red | Daffodil | Cobalt | Marmalade | Citron | Grape | Licorice | Eggshell | Pewter |
| Cherry | Gold | Cornflower | Peach | Emerald | Heather | Obsidian | Ghost | Silver |
| Chili | Goldenrod | Cyan | Persimmon | Forest | Hyacinth | Onyx | Glacier | Slate |
| Cinnabar | Lemon | Indigo | Pumpkin | Grass | Hydrangea | | Ice | Smoke |
| Claret | Marigold | Lapis | Salmon | Hunter | Iris | | Ivory | Steel |
| Crimson | Mustard | Midnight | Tangerine | Jade | Lavender | | Linen | Stone |
| Flame | Nugget | Peacock | | Kelly | Lilac | | Pearl | |
| Maroon | Ochre | Periwinkle | | Lime | Mauve | | Porcelain | |
| Paprika | Sun | Prussian | | Mint | Orchid | | Snow | |
| Raspberry | Sunflower | Robin's egg | | Moss | Plum | | Titanium white | |
| Rose | | Royal | | Olive | Puce | | Vanilla | |
| Rouge | | Sea | | Pine | Thistle | | | |
| Ruby | | Sky | | Pistachio | Violet | | | |
| Scarlet | | Steel | | Sage | | | | |
| Terra-cotta | | Surf | | Seafoam | | | | |
| Tomato | | Teal | | Terre verte | | | | |
| Wine | | Turquoise | | Viridian | | | | |

Enodnevna
zgodba
Rdeče
kapice

12:10

In the *Red Riding Hood* book, left color is used to tell stories. In this modern interpretation of the fairy tale, the dominant color changes from red (or "no") to green (or "yes") in the course of an evening when the heroine meets her wolf.
**Andreja Celigoj**

The colors of nature were used to tell the story of *Nature Unveiled* and reposition the chemical giant International Flavors & Fragrances. The company was perceived as old and stodgy, so the designers created a fresh approach. Rather than focus on the end product, which is mass manufactured and distributed by a large corporation, the designers built the brand around nature, the source of these products. Close-up photographs of natural forms, flowers and fruits, create a softer story for the company.
**Powell**

Chapter 7

# Case Studies

# Sean Adams
**Los Angeles, USA**

In 2014, Sean Adams embarked on a new chapter after twenty years with AdamsMorioka. He founded a new consultancy and studio, Adams, and the online publication, *Burning Settlers Cabin*. The focus of this studio is primarily pro-bono, educational, and non-profit work. Its philosophy is optimism and design for good, with a dash of kindness, generosity, and compassion. The work is pared down to essential elements and forms. This isn't minimalism for the sake of style. The goal is to clarify the message, respect the viewer, and slice through the visual chaos of the world.

Adams' work is unapologetically populist. "The solutions should be accessible to everyone," he states, "I don't want only three people at an avant-garde gallery to understand the message." He achieves this goal with simple forms, legible typography, and seductive color. For Adams, good design speaks to the best and highest level rather than the lowest common denominator. A wide range of viewers can understand a complex issue when the design solution is clear.

Color is integral to Adams' work. Purposeful and bold color combinations challenge expectations. His palettes are pure and geared toward impact using maximum contrast.

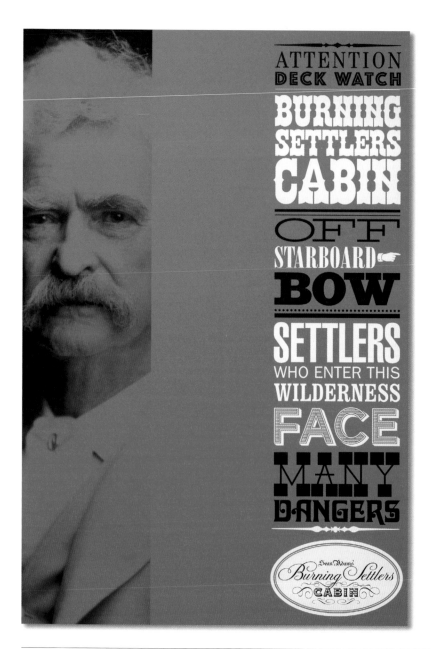

The first promotional poster for Burning Settlers Cabin is limited to three colors, white, black and turquoise. The eclectic typography is complex and multiple colors would create a barrier of color and letterforms. The turquoise also overprints the face of Mark Twain, creating a clear hierarchy between the words and imagery.

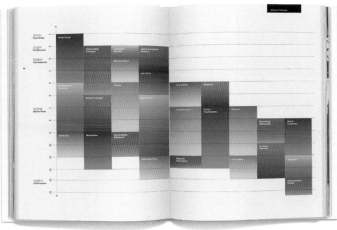

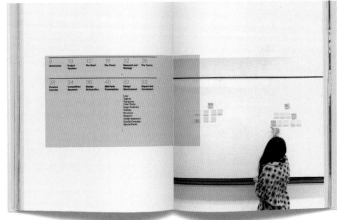

The Get Out The Vote campaign is an ongoing AIGA initiative to promote voting during important election years. The message here, vote, or be led like sheep, required a strong punch of color. The solid orange red and simple typography make the message straightforward. Too many colors would lead to a stylistic "candy store" communication. Two colors leave no doubt that this is an issue that should be addressed with no nonsense.

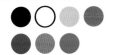

Spreads from the book, Connective Tissue, document the creative process to design a new strategy, identity, and campaign for the Arthritis Foundation. Headed by DesignMatters, the clear message from the client was to communicate the seriousness of arthritis' many forms, but focus on a positive life-affirming message. The vibrant color palette, taken from the final identity system, is woven through the book.

When he employs bright colors, he pushes the
boundaries beyond traditional good taste. Alternatively, black and white is punctuated with only one
color such as red or blue. Color is also derived from
the materials. On the project, 1955, designed for
AIGA's 100th anniversary, the color of canvas, felt,
buttons, and embroidery is not manipulated. It is an
honest representation of the materials, following the
Bauhaus concept; let materials be what they are.

"Do not use the default swatches," is a constant
message in the studio, or at ArtCenter where Adams
is at the helm of the graduate program. He creates
his own palettes and saves them for later use. These
palettes are taken from the natural world, architecture, film, and physical artifacts. The result is a
library of unexpected combinations that maintain
harmony. "I take photos everywhere and then sample the images. It's that easy," he explains.

Based in Los Angeles, Adams' color sense is closer
to Asian, Mexican, South American, and Polynesian
palettes than European ideals. These influences are
less muted or subtle. The bright light in Southern
California is also linked to this color sense. In a
landscape of harsh white sun almost 300 days a
year, it is inevitable that the colors are more saturated, intense, and bold. This, however, doesn't translate into garish or discordant. His use of contrast
and subtle shifts in a color maintain harmony.

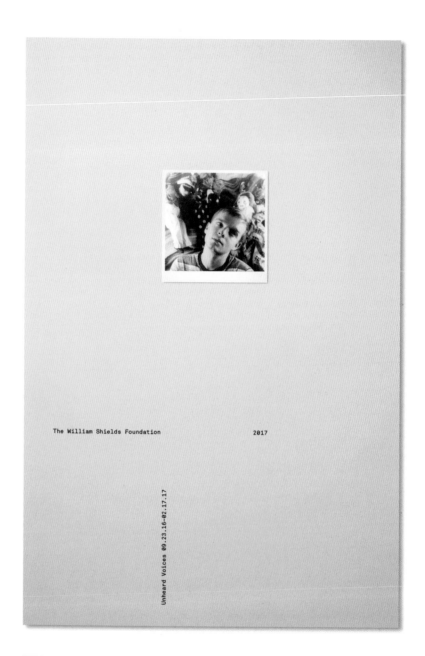

Typically, work for photography exhibitions steps back and
presents the images on a clean and neutral white background.
The William Shields Foundation supports under-represented
voices and Shield's work, *Other Voices,* his over 500 portraits
of gay and lesbian writers. The light pink references LGBT
community and makes clear that this is a different message
than a traditional poster for photography.

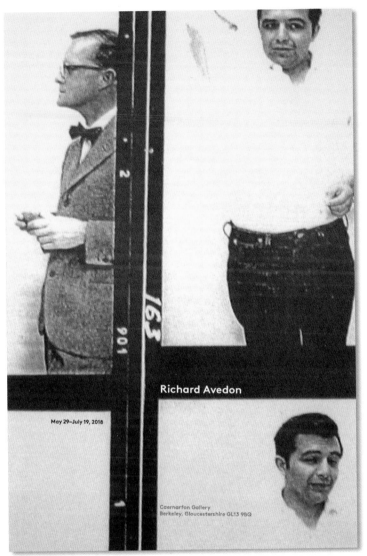

Richard Avedon

May 29–July 19, 2018

Caernarfon Gallery
Berkeley, Gloucestershire GL13 9BQ

**Art Center TestLab**
**Neo-Americana**
**November 20, 2013**
**14:00**

Bikini Berlin
Hardenbergplatz 2
7th Etage
10623 Berlin, Germany

**Die Herausforderung**
Erfinde und definiere eine Marke, die den
Amerikanischen Traum für eine neue
Generation von Europäern übersetzt. Finde
neue Bedeutungspotentiale angesichts des
aktuellen problematischen Rufs Amerikas:
NSA, Irak und Guantanemo Bay.

**Das Ergebnis**
Drei Kreativteams aus Kalifornien präsentieren
in den Bereichen Kultur, Reisen und
Unterhaltung jeweils eine neue Marke, die eine
Faszination für amerikanischen Nonkonformis-
mus neu entfachen soll. Bei der heutigen
Genration Berliner Millennials.

Supported by BIKINI BERLIN and Berlin Partner

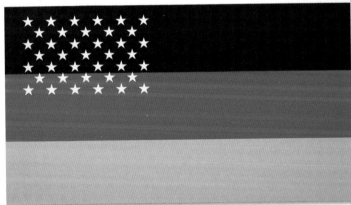

The poster for an exhibition of work from Richard Avedon
presents a detail from the contact sheet of Truman Capote
and Perry Smith. Capote was writing In Cold Blood, an account of Smith's brutal murder of the Clutter family in Kansas. The black edges of the photographs act as a prison and
separate Capote and Smith. The yellow tint shifts to green,
creating an uneasy tension.

Designed for a presentation on the state of American culture
in contemporary Germany, the poster and invitations use colors from the German flag as a clear signifier, but subvert the
information with stars from the American flag. This disjoint,
expecting to see red, white, and blue, or only the German flag,
force the viewer to see both, in his or her head. This creates a
more intimate message.

As part of the identity and signage program for Stein Eye at UCLA, designed at AdamsMorioka, the signs are color coded to direct the viewer to different buildings. Each building's exterior signage follows the coded color shown here. As a pre-eminent center for eye care, the goal was to create an easy to see approach relying on color and shape first, then the verbiage. The colors were chosen for visibility and interaction with the Richard Meier architecture.

High School Programs:
Drop-in, Footsteps to College,
SAT Prep

**578** participants total

**12th graders**

Seniors typically take advantage of our regular drop-in programs, and this year was no different. The lion's share of seniors visited to work on college applications, personal statements, signing up for the SAT/ACT, and financial aid forms. Other popular services included completing scholarship applications, assessing financial aid packages, and signing up for college placement exams.

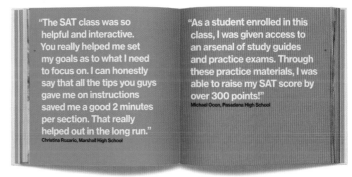

"The SAT class was so helpful and interactive. You really helped me set my goals as to what I need to focus on. I can honestly say that all the tips you guys gave me on instructions saved me a good 2 minutes per section. That really helped out in the long run."
Christina Rozario, Marshall High School

"As a student enrolled in this class, I was given access to an arsenal of study guides and practice exams. Through these practice materials, I was able to raise my SAT score by over 300 points!"
Michael Ocon, Pasadena High School

We've added more zest to our zeal.

"I LOVE CAP!!"
Jessica Bernal, Muir High School

**<3"**

President's Message

2014-2015 was a big year for CAP, and for me personally. As an organization CAP added a wonderful board member who has had deep connections to CAP as an organization and has supported CAP for years. CAP reached a new height of serving 950 students, helped graduating seniors earn more than $700,000 dollars in scholarships, and saw hundreds of students from our programs enroll in their best fit colleges.

We also closed the year on strong fiscal ground, poised to continue this work and ensure that if they want to, any student in Pasadena can go to college. On a personal note, I got married and started a family of my own. The kinds of life altering events that make you think about the future. I know that being a part of CAP, and contributing to our mission of seeing all of our students achieve success, will help make our community the kind place that I want for my family. I am proud to be a part of CAP now and look forward to what CAP will continue to do in the future.
Sam Galloro, President

CAP reached a new height of serving 950 students, helped graduating seniors earn more than $700,000 dollars in scholarships.

Alumni Program:
I Heart College

**189** Returning Alumni

**56** New Alumni

**54** Colleges and Universities Represented

College Access Plan is a non-profit organization that helps high school students, who would typically not have the support, to apply for and enter college. the Annual Report communicates CAP's mission and attitude. Fun, but not frivolous, was the driving force to use blunt and simple messages from students and information about programs, but to add spice and fun with a technicolor color palette.

**Practicing graphic design is a process of creating change. Change made by designers committed to great ideas: to See, Do and Lead.**

ArtCenter's MFA Graduate Graphic Design (MGx) program educates graphic designers who will lead the next global generation of our profession, influence companies, communities and society at large, and extend the boundaries of communication design in all directions.

Expanding upon the College's internationally recognized undergraduate Graphic Design curriculum, this MFA program will immerse you in craft, design leadership and strategic thought in equal measures, all within a socially-responsible transmedia platform that includes print, interaction, motion, packaging and mediatecture. We emphasize entrepreneurship, leadership, and management with a focus on practical, yet exquisite, professional design solutions.

Our regular two-year program consists of four full terms plus a Summer term reserved for a studio independent study, plus an internship. If appropriate, we also offer a three-year program that includes two additional terms of undergraduate Graphic Design courses tailored to meet your needs.

Aligned with our ethos of mixing the practical and exquisite, this Multi-Tool provides straightforward, and clear information for the designer.

It can also serve as a ruler.

*Sean Adams*
**Sean Adams**
Director

**Nik Hafermaas**
Chair

GRAPHIC DESIGN GRADUATE PROGRAM    **3**

The viewbook for the ArtCenter Graphic Design graduate program avoids the traditional tricks of college viewbooks, multi-racial students playing frisbee on the quad. The book serves as a useful tool with quotes from A-list designers serving on the program's advisory board, rulers, anatomy of letterforms, and other pages of actual information. The color talks to the school's location, Southern California, and its vibrant energy.

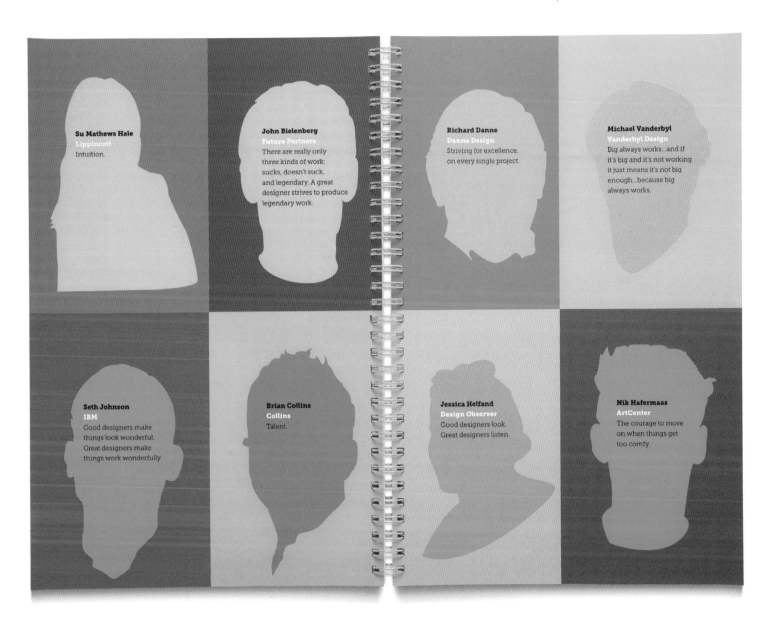

**Su Mathews Hale**
**Lippincott**
Intuition.

**John Bielenberg**
**Future Partners**
There are really only
three kinds of work:
sucks, doesn't suck,
and legendary. A great
designer strives to produce
legendary work.

**Richard Danne**
**Danne Design**
Striving for excellence,
on every single project.

**Michael Vanderbyl**
**Vanderbyl Design**
Big always works...and if
it's big and it's not working
it just means it's not big
enough...because big
always works.

**Seth Johnson**
**IBM**
Good designers make
things look wonderful.
Great designers make
things work wonderfully

**Brian Collins**
**Collins**
Talent.

**Jessica Helfand**
**Design Observer**
Good designers look.
Great designers listen.

**Nik Hafermaas**
**ArtCenter**
The courage to move
on when things get
too comfy.

# Brand New School

## Santa Monica/New York, USA

Brand New School (BNS), a live action and design company, responds to visual culture all over the world, translating it into television commercials, music videos, and on-air network identity packages. BNS has evolved in a very short time from boutique shop to major player in on-air television broadcast design and commercial production. Founded in 2000 by Jonathan Notaro, later joined by typography master Jens Gehlhaar, the firm has offices on both United States coasts.

Notaro founded BNS to be a creative boutique that he describes as "a bit off center, where we're comfortable." He is determined to create a new school of thought that extends design beyond a mere typographical experience. The firm is immersed in visual style in both printed media and motion pictures, and the designers are deeply aware of the importance of knowing how the viewer is affected. Notaro says, "The key is to put together a group of creative people, give them the freedom to do their thing, and keep it fun, even during ninety-hour weeks."

The play principle may be key, and the work exhibits strong innovation. BNS has successfully negotiated a tough balancing act between the demands of advertising clients and producing thoughtful, striking work. "As graphic designers, we're telling a story, and at the end of the day, it's more involving to see performance than flying type." One of the key elements used in BNS narratives is color.

This was Mudd Jeans' first commercial, which aired exclusively on MTV. Meant to appeal to teenage girls, the spot communicates the large variety of washes and textures available. BNS shot a dancing model in front of a green screen. Later everything was erased but the jeans. The pants appear to take a journey through fantastic environments in a cross between a storybook cartoon world and a hip dance video. The various environments dictated the color palettes, all highly saturated and using the full spectrum of color.

BNS created this show package for ABC TV's new evening programming look. The piece visually illustrates "the idea of getting more from the evening than you'd expect" by playing off the circle shape of the logo. The animation of the logo, circles, a talk bubble, and a plus sign have an interesting personality. A bright, playful palette of high-key colors is used, with a bright lime green background chosen because of its contrast with the ABC trademark colors of black and, alternatively, bright international yellow. The green conveys the message of a variety of television content and is refreshingly different as an on-air ID for the network.

"We really don't have a color philosophy. I guess our use of color started as being a bit more pop-ish and fun rather than muted and serious," explains Jonathan Notaro. "Subtleties in color don't necessarily translate well on television." So BNS' color choices tend to be brighter colored. Notaro continues, "This is partly due to the amount of humor in our work. A brighter palette seems to enforce that not-so-serious attitude."

Brand New School tends toward a more optimistic color palette that is hip and masculine. Pop culture elements are fused with parody modes of contemporary art. All design aspects reflect the contradictory ideas of modern life. "I think we have a deeper understanding of design history than many companies that evolved from street culture," creative director Gelhaar comments, "which keeps the work as intelligent as it is creative."

While conceptually driven, theirs is a highly technical as well as aesthetically demanding medium. Notaro explains, "Most of the time we are concerned about getting our ideas figured out in terms of narrative and visual arts. This is due mainly to having short deadlines, and color usually isn't something that is heavily scrutinized. Colors are just about the last thing we think about, or should I say, are conscious of, on a project."

This spot for Fox's Fuel TV Network creates an action-based film language that is visually stunning. In B-movie style, a helmeted biker and his pack of Motocrossers rid the world of giant ant aliens before flying and stunting into the sunset, leaving mankind safe once more. The color palette is a desaturated 16mm grainy cheap-feeling film look. The image appears worn and damaged, with film angles mirroring the spirit of 1950s sci-fi.

For this music video, director Chris Appelbaum took the band American Hi-Fi to Hays, Kansas; threw a party at a fan's house; and let the cameras roll. With a punk rock attitude, BNS then designed five segments made to look like a high school student's scrapbook come to life. The piece explores rock and roll iconography without a tight graphic system; it is meant to seem made by multiple hands. The only structure imposed is the use of felt-tipped markers and ballpoint pens, which provide the color scheme as well.

Muse's "Hysteria" music video needed to be a breakthrough piece to reach American audiences. To match the hysteria of the song, brain abstraction graphics and visual hemorrhages of thought images leave the band submerged in a red cloud of bloodlike color. All color is desaturated, with skin tones preserved to make the band feel alive. Overall, the dark melancholic red creates an aggressive emotional feeling.

# Chimera Design
## St. Kilda, Victoria, Australia

Chimera Design, established in 1997 by creative director John Magart, provides expertise for a diverse range of clients. The studio thrives on challenging projects and is focused on achieving unique outcomes in a diverse array of media. The designers constantly push the bounds of print and multimedia. Chimera believes that great design needs a strong conceptual base and point of difference. Color often provides the difference.

In response to questions about their color philosophy, designer Keelie Teasdale speaks for Chimera. "One's reaction to color is very personal and affected by social trends, styles, or conditioning, yet we as designers must create color combinations that have a concentrated impact on the majority of people." Chimera understands that changing color schemes in a particular design can create very different emotional responses. Teasdale continues, "Color defines the mood of the project. It subconsciously conveys the base feeling of the object you are designing for. It is the visual link to the core emotion of the job. It is imperative, therefore, to choose colors wisely." As each project's demands are different, Chimera believes it is impossible to work with a constant palette. "There are no rules to the amount of colors a job should use. Certain jobs demand full color usage, while others gain their impact from one carefully chosen spot color," says Teasdale. "Our key to choosing colors is breaking down the brief to its key emotional values.

Tabcorp's introduction of a new betting game, *Mystery6,* into the Australian entertainment industry had to capture the carnival atmosphere of sporting fun, remain intriguing, and appeal to a broad market, especially the youth audience. Propelled off the page by magenta, the mysterious nature evokes festive excitement. The purple hues offer subtle hints of an ethereal nature, and it is these hues, often linked with good fortune and intuition, that add a sophistication and grounding to their dominant partner.

Victoria's State Netball Hockey Centre is a premier sporting facility located in the heart of Melbourne's sporting district. As part of their branding, they requested three murals designed to support and extend the facility's new corporate identity. Carried from the identity through to the wall graphics, the three colors accompanied by white are distinctly Australian in feel and are used to represent the stadium's three key aspects: red for management, blue for netball, and green for hockey. As high-chroma colors, they are clear, distinctive, and dynamic. The chosen colors allow white to stand proudly, lightening and opening up the design. Combined with linear graphics and bitmap photography, the colors intensify notions of movement and sporting passion.

These points can be translated into their color equivalents. Depending on the desired emotion, these colors can be anything from vibrant, powerful, or exuberant to lively, youthful, or welcoming. Each can capture attention and stimulate emotion, reflect comfort or even sterility." The firm considers an emotional point of view, leveraging color associations and resulting psychological effects.

At Chimera, the process of color selection is fairly systematic. Teasdale explains, "After detecting the core color, we either harness it as a standalone; combine it with its monochromatic breakdowns; or introduce a holding, achromatic, contrasting, clashing, or complementary color. It is often in the combination of colors that we create the perfect design combination. The power of color creates impact and drive, where the base color acts as a means to showcase its partner while adding depth and stability."

aquacon2001

Aquacon is a conference and trade show for all sectors of the Australian aquatic industry. The identity was created to appear as if viewed through water. It has a slightly distorted perspective that implies constant movement and reflection. Color enhances this sense of movement through the use of analogous blues seen through each other. These cool colors, although refreshing and meditative in themselves, together create a whirlpool of youthful, effervescent energy.

**ARTISTIC DIRECTOR'S REPORT 1999**

The annual report for Dancehouse was an opportunity to create a document that matched the dynamic, innovative, and diverse nature of a progressive dance company. The goal was to evoke contrary emotional reactions in the reader, much like that of a viewer of contemporary dance. Fluorescent red, pale blue, and opaque white were chosen either to neutralize or intensify the corporate black throughout the piece. Printed over a mixture of four natural-toned stocks, the colors are intensified or subdued through their interaction with the paper. This combination of vivid, powerful red, often brash and almost assaulting; a refreshing pale blue, adding restraint; and a white that conveys calm through intricate detail create a pace within the book that exudes energy.

# Dynamo
## Dublin, Ireland

Dynamo, established in 1992, is one of Ireland's most respected design consultancies, combining award-winning design with intuitive strategic thinking. Since its inception, the firm has developed expert creative skills to meet the diverse requirements of its varied client base. It has added new skills, new technologies, new people, and new thinking to evolve into a hybrid communications company. Dynamo does print and brand identity, motion graphics, interactive design, and packing for consumer brands.

"We want to create communication programs that enhance brand performance. And we achieve consistent results by adopting an intuitive, strategic approach to brand communications. That means strategy borne out of common sense and instinct rather than a fixed restrictive process," says creative director Jamie Helly. As a result of this philosophy, Dynamo creates memorable and engaging work for a variety of industries and audiences.

Dynamo's use of color adds a new dimension to corporate communications and packaging. Its work in consumer products uses color in way that facilitates awareness and recall. Its bright, clear palettes evoke an emotional response, subliminal at times, that suggests the need for something new in a consumer's mind. Dynamo makes effective use of limited colors as well as full-color higher-budget projects. Color works especially hard in its designs to grab attention and keep it.

Although it owned a large share of the Irish snack food market for some years, Tayto was losing ground to new market entrants such as Pringles and Walkers and feeling pressure from fragmentation in the snack food marketplace. Dynamo's comprehensive rebranding pushes Mr. Tayto, the figurative mascot of the brand, to center stage. The new packaging introduces a smile device to the color scheme and graphic elements that maximize the brand's accessibility and friendly personality. Designs for the packages predominantly feature the primary colors red, yellow, and blue. These colors work with a few accent hues to give the snack foods high-impact shelf appeal. Tayto witnessed steady growth after the redesign, with market share increasing from 43 to 50 percent. Tayto marketing director PJ Brigdale says, "The new packaging design has created far-reaching potential for the Tayto brand, influencing a host of promotional opportunities we hadn't considered before." There is a bold simplicity in the Tayto packaging that is enhanced by high-visibility color palettes.

As Yoplait's brand consultants, Dynamo was given the task of creating a new identity for the reformulated replacement for an ailing diet brand. Dynamo responded with a new brand name, Yoplait 0%, to maximize shelf presence. The labels are color-coded and utilize photos that correspond to product ingredients. This colorway system creates a delicious-looking range of products with clearly distinguished flavors, making consumer selection easy.

Honest is a new snack offering from Tayto. This product responds to consumer insights charting the trends toward more convenient, healthy offerings. Tayto went one better by creating a premium healthy snack, previously nonexistent in the Irish and UK snack markets. Dynamo eschewed the usual Technicolor approach to snack packaging, instead adopting a blanched color scheme. White is a not often seen in this hugely competitive food category, so its use lends significant visibility in a crowded store environment. The package's design takes on an editorial style that breaks rules and attracts discerning, health-conscious consumers.

The Lucas Bols group is a subsidiary of Remy Cointreau SA, the global liqueur distillery. Bols approached Dynamo with an ambitious brief for creating a new brand identity for their innovative *Total Cocktail's* idea. The initiative is designed to provide advice, training, and supplier contacts for people interested in selling and serving alcoholic cocktails. The innovative offer allowed Bols to assume ownership of cocktail-making itself, enabling promotion of their wide range of cocktail mix liqueurs. Dynamo's work for Bols includes a pocket-sized bartender's handbook and sales presentation materials. The design for Total Cocktails suggests the alchemy of drinks and ice. The visual style is reminiscent of 1950s cocktail lounges blended with contemporary typography. The Bols *Total Cocktail's* booklet uses a palette of vivid colors to signpost the book's extensive index of cocktail recipes. Full-colored solid backgrounds are used throughout to bookmark popular cocktails. The Cosmopolitan, for example, is set against a bright pink.

## ZOMBIE

**total cocktails**

### TASTE

SOUR — SWEET
WEAK — STRONG

### INGREDIENTS

½ shot light rum
½ shot gold rum
½ shot dark rum
½ shot dry orange curaçao liqueur
½ shot apricot brandy liqueur
½ shot grenadine
1 shot freshly-squeezed lime juice
2 ½ shots orange juice
2 ½ shots pineapple juice
¼ shot 151° rum

### TOOLS
Shaker, strainer

### GLASS
Hurricane

### TECHNIQUE
Shake first 9 ingredients with ice and strain. Top with 151° rum.

### ICE
Serve over ice cubes

### GARNISH
Pineapple wedge

# Stillhart Konzept
## Zurich, Switzerland

Martin Stillhart founded Stillhart Konzept in 2011. the firm's activities encompass a broad range of media and types of clients: corporate design, editorial design, organization and implementation of websites, exhibition graphics, and signage. Martin Stillhart's experiences at Basel School of Art with noted typographer, Wolfgang Weingart, is evident in the solutions. While many firms may deny craft and focus only on brand and image, Stillhart Konzept manages complex communications with a refined and poetic typographic language. They don't shy away from perfection and excellence in craft, but embrace it with flawlessly executed work.

The firm's use of color is bold and intense. Imagery, typography, and backgrounds are treated equally with the same exuberant spirit. The same palettes are played out across all media, from print to the screen to exhibitions and 3-dimensional design.

Before founding Stillhart Konzept, Martin Stillhart was a partner at the internationally recognized firm, Fauxpas Grafik. He worked abroad with Designers Republic in Sheffield, Landor Associates in San Francisco, and Atelier Lars Müller in Baden. This range of experience is one of the reasons for the firm's success.

Although Stillhart Konzept professes no specific color philosophy, it is evident that less is more. Many print projects often use two colors. Red and black are a frequently used combination. But there is no unnecessary form or color in the work. Every part of a composition has a function and creates a clear statement.

*Feinschliff
Arbeit, die Chancen schafft

### 3. Pfiffige Produkte und Dienstleistungen

Anspruchsvoll: Bewusst wagen wir uns in Geschäftsberei-che, welche hohe Anforderungen an eine Sozialfirma stel-len. Freude an hochwertigen Dienstleistungen, an schö-nen Materialien und ihrer gekonnten Verarbeitung sowie an Gestaltungsspielraum belohnen uns und treiben uns an.

5

Feinhiten is a social enterprise committed, to work with unemployed people to achieve concrete improvements. Depending on previous knowledge, skills, and experience, individuals are hired to work in bookbinding, woodworking and furniture restoration, screen printing and labeling, textiles or upholstery. Stillhart's design for a promotional booklet stakes a clear claim with the company name and phrase "Arbeit, die Chancen schafft," or in English, "labor which creates opportunities." Red is used as a device to stop the viewer and demand attention. The raw materials and unsentimental photography reinforce the authenticity and honesty of the brand.

Designed for the Swiss Heritage Society, *Public Areas of Switzerland* addresses how the quality of life in our towns and cities is closely associated with the public space. Squares and parks, town centers and lakefront are meeting places and places of recreation. Stillhart Konzept's design for this publication utilizes color sparingly, with a simple red image on the cover and few four color images inside. The combination of blunt typography, black, and red color communicate the seriousness of the issue.

The exhibition *Posada to Alÿs. Mexican Art from 1900 Until Today* at Kunsthaus Zurich examines contemporary art of Mexico and the beginnings of social criticism printmaking. Stillhart designed a suite of materials for the exhibition: a publication on newsprint, the signage, and the exhibition poster. The yellow backround and one color printing in red recall quickly and cheaply produced activist posters in Mexico, with an overlay of refined typography and form.

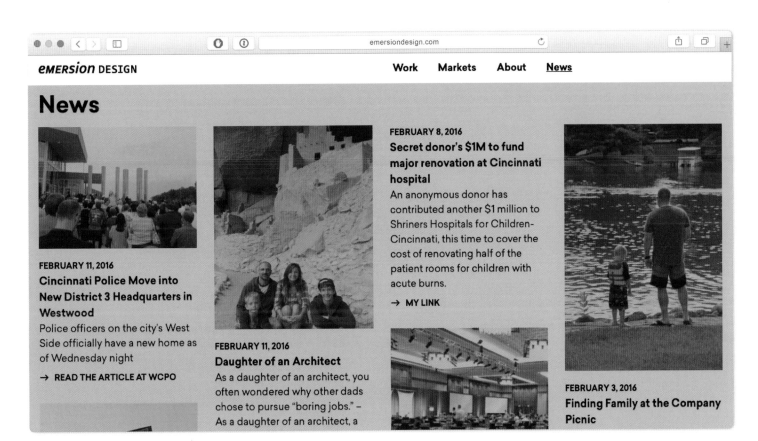

Emersion Design is an architecture firm working with clients interested in design for good, with a goal to raise the quality of life and society. They accomplish this through beautiful, strategic, cost effective and highly sustainable spaces, buildings and master plans. Stillhart avoids two clichés. First there are no shades of natural green signifying "sustainable."

Second, the imagery integrates people, rather than only sterile images of buildings. The restraint of typography and the simple application of turquoise create a dynamic solution. Large four color images of buildings on a subtle color palette might read as elitist and about luxury. But Stillhart, maintains an elegant minimalism that reminds the viewer of the firm's goals, to help society.

# Green Dragon Office
## Los Angeles, USA

The Green Dragon Office is led by its founder and creative director Lorraine Wild. As a designer, writer, critic, lecturer, and faculty member of the Program in Graphic Design at California Institute of the Arts (CalArts), Wild has been a highly influential figure to scores of students, teachers, practitioners, and thinkers in the field of graphic design. Her firm, Green Dragon Office, is a collaborative studio that designs publications, identities, websites, posters, signage, and other communication media for clients ranging from museums to schools, publishers, corporations, and nonprofit organizations of all types.

The San Francisco Museum of Modern Art notes, "Lorraine Wild produces graphic designs that have the effortless grace of information that falls into place. She is a master of Modernism who champions sparse, abstract design disciplined by an invisible grid." As a designer, Wild is probably best known for books. Green Dragon Office continues to design books as well as broaden the scope of projects. Wild explains, "Underpinning our work is an obsession with direct collaboration with artists, architects, writers, editors, and curators. Our work is diverse because we strive to keep our process free of preconceptions. We try to create communication that reflects the intelligence and spirit of our collaborations, which are specific to each project. We translate those ideas into forms that audiences will remember and appreciate."

For the architectural firm Marmol Radziner and Associates, the designers represented the firm with a mix of slick high-end technology elements, such as high-tech type; silver inks; and earthy, crafty elements such as the textured stock.

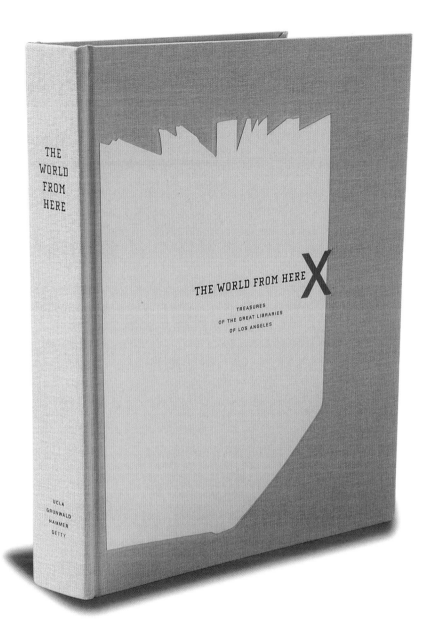

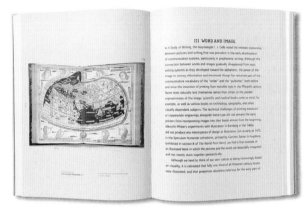

This book accompanies the exhibition *The World from Here: Treasures of the Great Libraries of Los Angeles.* The exhibition features a collection of rare books, letters, and manuscripts and encourages a deeper understanding of how these important artifacts represent the history of ideas. For the book design, Lorraine Wild breaks the large volume into sections.

Each section is dominated by a desaturated tint. Journeying through the material, the neighboring section shifts to the next hue positioned on the color wheel. The designers use book silhouettes both on the cover, above left, and throughout as a unifying element.

Lorraine Wild says about her philosophy of color usage, "Color can go beyond decoration and instead can be used as a structural element that helps organize the page. A good example is the shifting color backgrounds in *The World from Here* book [pictured on page 165] or the use of dark brown to indicate archival material in Mike Kelly's *The Uncanny* [opposite page]. Those [color] decisions are driven not by aesthetics but from a need to communicate something about the content of the book."

Color is used as part of a set of design elements that often includes diverse typefaces, disparate layouts, unusual images, and dense bodies of text. Together these elements can form logical and beautiful relationships in service to content and meaning. When asked about using a recognizable color palette in the work, Wild responds, "We stay away from primary colors, except for the occasional blast of PMS warm red on a book design. I'm interested in more complex color relationships than the high-contrast effects associated with primaries."

These philosophical approaches seem to be working. Wild's designs are responsive and stand out for their subtlety in a communications-saturated world. Designer Laurie Haycock Makela, a former CalArts colleague, summarizes, "I admire her work because it speaks for many cultural institutions of our time in alternating fits of elegance and anarchy."

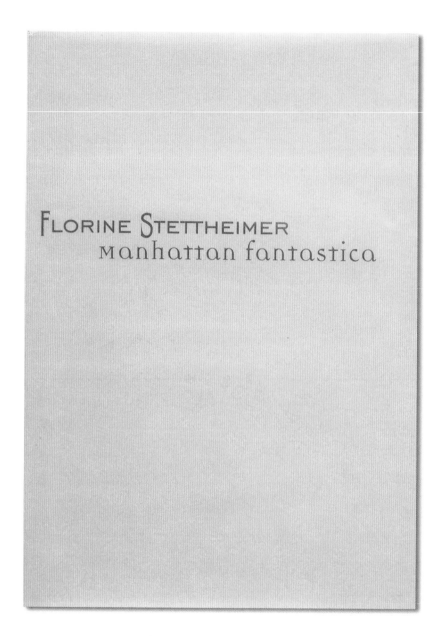

FLORINE STETTHEIMER
manhattan fantastica

The cover of a book about artist Florine Stettheimer's *Manhattan Fantastica* series of paintings and drawings was the first time Wild was able to allude to an artist's work rather than simply display a piece of art. The designer used hot pink printed on the book cover and an orange-colored doily pattern printed on a translucent overlay dust jacket to achieve a strange color effect not typical of offset printing.

*The Uncanny*, by Mike Kelly, is the restaging of an exhibition in the 1990s and the second version of this book. The essay from the first book is reprinted here with a brown frame and brown type (upper right). The images from the first book are reprinted in fake sepia (lower left), while new images are printed in color (upper left and lower right). The effect is an organic unity holding the odd collection together.

# Johnson banks
## London, UK

Johnson banks provides creative and pragmatic solutions to communications problems in a smart and lively way. Its interpretations produce designs that keep clients' brands fresh and in the public consciousness. Looking at the firm's work gives a sense that there is thinking behind the graphics.

What might be especially unexpected in the work of Johnson banks is its use of color. If designers are influenced by the region of the world in which they live, then creative director Michael Johnson's color palettes are not what should be, given the grayness of London. His work typically features pure vivid colors, often jewel toned. The brightness of his choices make color a powerful tool in causing the firm's work to stand out in cluttered environments, both physical and printed.

Johnson banks uses color purposefully. There is a sense of clear color harmonies and unusual associations, such as the integration of sound and color, as used in the Science Museum wayfinding system shown on page 168.

For one of the preeminent British design companies, Johnson banks has a very un-stereotypically British notion of color. Perhaps it is because Johnson has worked around the world, incorporating the influences of Sydney, Melbourne, Tokyo, and New York, as well as the worlds of advertising and design into his work.

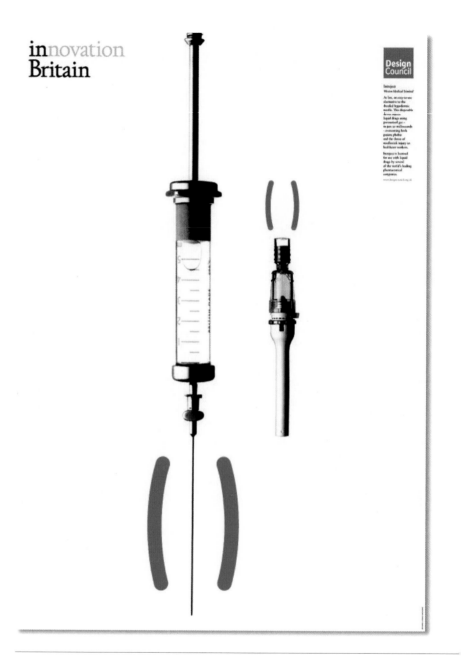

The British Design Council wanted a set of posters featuring some of the 1,000-odd products that were part of its Millennium Products campaign. For a multi-language audience Johnson banks used pictures and symbols that any person of any culture could read or at least decode. This minimally colored poster highlights the imagery, providing a focused experience for the viewer.

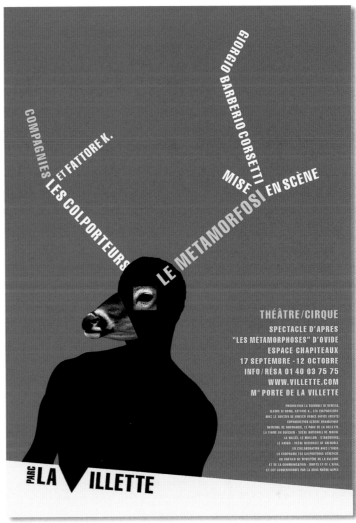

"How do you evolve a favorite French cultural institution? Let them own the edges of everything they do," explains Johnson for Parc de la Villette's solution. The client needed a link to the old identity, but a nod to the future. Johnson banks created an identity device—a black border graphic running along the edge of every piece of print the client develops. The designers also imposed limitations: one typeface and a single, powerful image. *"Découvrez le jardin des cultures"* (Discover the garden of cultures) is a promotion for the Parc. "Our thought was to take the grass of the park and use it to make iconic images, so grass becomes a linking idea," says Johnson. The *Métamorphoses* poster is for a theater event at the Parc. The pure, bold blue attracts the eye and speaks of clear blue skies.

The new Welcome Wing extension to the Science Museum in London overwhelms the senses with its vast, dark, cathedral-like space. The space is crammed to the gills with state-of-the-art examples of twenty-first century science and technology, so the client needed a way to stop visitors from wandering around the wing like lost sheep and help them locate the things they wanted to see.

Johnson banks developed a set of self-illuminating beacons with pulsing letters and embedded sound chips, each with its own note, playing the music of the wing.

Whether standing on the third floor platform or in an entrance, visitors can work out where they are by a combination of color and sound. These wayfinding graphics utilize a series of jewel-toned colors against black backgrounds, mirroring the exhibition space itself and providing easy-to-read signage. With the darkened corridors of the wing, another level of signage was required, one that dealt with the nitty-gritty of getting from elevators to exhibitions, or deciding which way to go from decision points on stairs. The suite of self-illuminated signs is based on a cross section of the wing and further helps visitors navigate through the space.

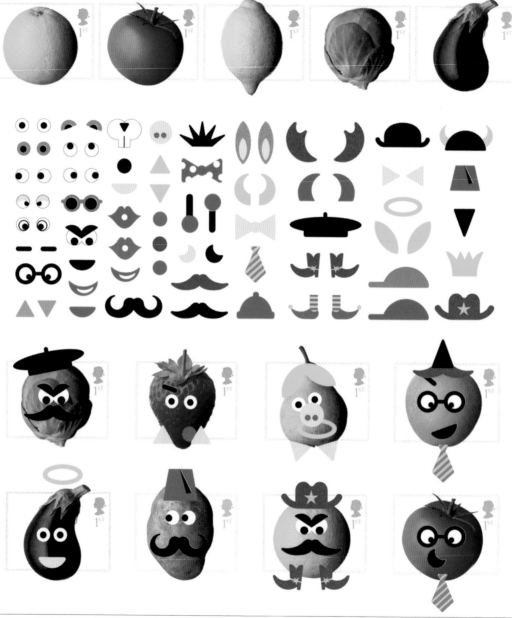

The Fruit and Veg stamps for the UK's Royal Mail are striking-ly original. The stamp kit contains ten stamps with illustra-tions of fruits and vegetables rendered in a classical realistic style, accompanied by seventy-six stickers of facial features and accessories that allow postal customers to produce their own personalized stamps. The brief was to create interactive stamps for children. The designers where inspired by the kids' game Mr. Potato Head. This fun piece again showcases the firm's preference for bright color palettes—the perfect recipe for an audience of children.

Making learning English fun, not exhausting, was the goal of this project. The 900-odd classrooms worldwide that the British Council uses to teach English are not the most inspiring of places. Combine that with a heavy session of conjunctive-auxiliary-phrasal-pronouns, and Johnson banks could see legions of keen young students falling into deep comas at their desks. After poring over English grammar books, the designers created forty classroom cards. Ten themes, such as conjugations of irregular verbs, were chosen, and simple, colorful designs that could be put on a wall or used in lessons were produced. Many cards utilize pairs of complementary colors to make them more active and engaging. Some of the comparative superlatives cards, such as "small" shown above, were banned in certain countries.

# Uwe Loesch
### Erkath, Germany

Uwe Loesch is an internationally recognized poster designer (*Plakatgestalter*) and professor at the Bergi University of Wuppertal in Düsseldorf. Although Professor Loesch works in a variety of media, including book and catalog design, identity establishment, and campaigns for social and cultural institutions, he is known best for his posters.

Loesch's posters have strong meanings and messages delivered with a minimalist approach. He does not have a predefined visual style. He works with intelligence, wit, strong contrast, and the interaction of words and images to raise awareness for a variety of sociopolitical causes. Growing up in postwar Germany affected the way Loesch perceives and transmits ideas. He adopted the poster early in his career as his medium for bringing about change.

Loesch's work philosophy is "I see more or less, never the less!" and he admits to being influenced by the nihilistic French art movement Dada. In response to our consumerism-saturated world, Loesch has said, "Wait a minute. If everyone keeps shouting louder and louder, no one will be able to hear, much less understand or believe, anything." As a result of this point of view, his work tends to whisper and actively engage the viewer in drawing conclusions. Whispering often results in restrained, clever typography and color usage.

This poster, called *Game Over* (*...und raus bist du*, ...and you are out) was created for the competition Children Are the Rhythm of the World, organized by the Deutsches Plakatmuseum Essen. The poster features the portrait of a young African soldier that has been color manipulated to take on the character of military camouflage. The blood-red typography—the subject of which is a German children's rhyme about the game hide-and-seek—overlays the image.

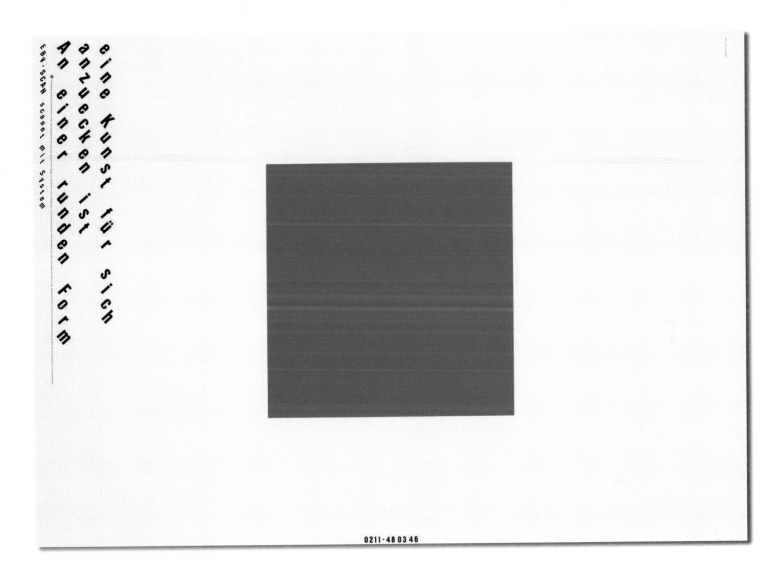

For EBV-scan Düsseldorf, a lithography company, Loesch created this poster to invite customers to a party for presenting new scanner technology imported from Japan. Loesch calls this poster *Squaring the Circle Is an Art Itself*, and the central image is a parody of the Japanese flag. The designer has squared the flag's red circle, placing it on a white field with spare typography.

Loesch uses color sparingly. He notes, "Color decorates, color irritates, color seduces, color makes you blind. Therefore, I prefer black on white." Loesch scrutinizes color photography images and determines whether they work in order to "celebrate the difference between the nature-beautiful and the art-beautiful."

Red is the color most present in Loesch's work. He believes it is the best auxiliary color to black-and-white, adding, "Red is synonymous with poster." Loesch occasionally uses fluorescent colors that he thinks are particularly suitable for signaling, and other color schemes if they are specific to the message and culture he is working with. However, because red is a symbol of a number of messages, he uses it often.

Loesch feels that color plays a crucial role in the communication process. "In the sequence of perception, color is noticed before the form. To see red without thinking red is not possible, at least in the Western world," says Loesch.

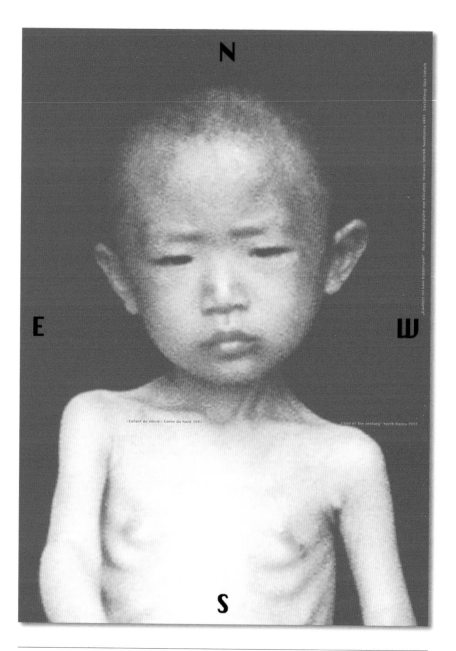

This poster was created for the exhibition Childhood Is Not a Children's Play, organized by the Deutsches Plakatmuseum Essen. Loesch calls this poster *Child of the Century*. It features the saturated image of a small starving child from North Korea. The designer uses red symbolically throughout his work to draw attention to social causes.

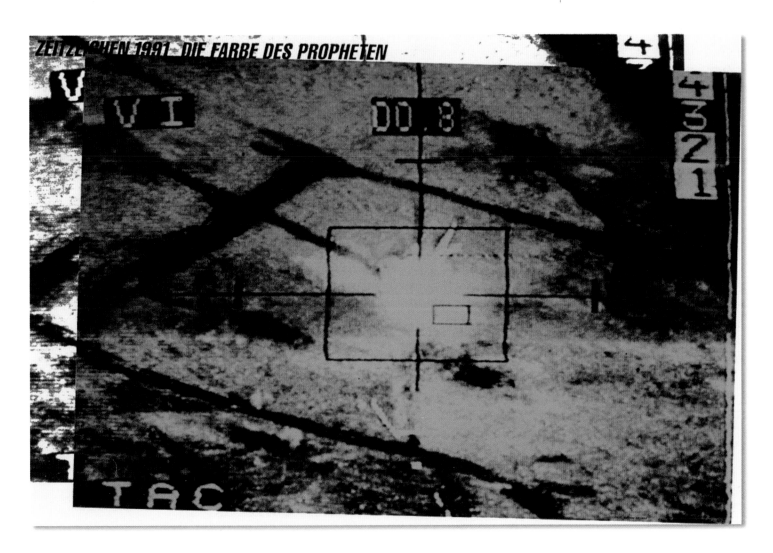

This poster was created during the first Gulf War. The designer uses the double exposure of repeating images taken from satellite weaponry gun sites. The blue over the black-and-white image simulates night and conveys a sense of foreboding. It is an example of what has been referred to as Loesch's "strategy of irritation," in which he deliberately causes a shift in perception by using very small changes in the expected presentation of his graphic elements.

# Lorenc + Yoo Design
## Atlanta, USA

Lorenc + Yoo Design is an Atlanta-based environmental graphic design firm whose projects include retail spaces, tradeshow exhibits, furniture design, wayfinding signage, museum exhibitions, and event and corporate visitor center environmental graphics. Partners Jan Lorenc and Chung Youl Yoo came from very different cultural backgrounds. Lorenc emigrated to the United States from Poland as a boy, while Yoo immigrated more recently from Korea via Paraguay. Together they work within a wide range of stylistic environments and vocabularies for a variety of clients.

Lorenc + Yoo Design's philosophy is one of exploration, inquisitiveness, and commitment to innovation. Its approach centers on collaboration among design disciplines, allowing each client's persona to come through in the executed design. Lorenc + Yoo Design teams include architects; interior, industrial, and graphic designers; and a cadre of specific consultants assembled to meet the needs of a given project. They share ideas, ask questions, and engage in constructive criticism among the disciplines in order to achieve an integrated design solution.

Lorenc and Yoo believe in design as narration; they tell client and brand stories through the environments that they create. The designers use color as an important element. Partner Jan Lorenc explains, "The color needs to narrate the focus of the space. Your journey through the space can be packaged by pieces of content wrapped in a focal color that evolves with the content."

The Palladium Company develops urban centers that are prime destinations for shopping, residences, and entertainment. This is its exhibit for industry conventions. Finishes, materials, and colors are all inspired by Palladium's development and construction styles. The exhibit is a modern classic, dominated by blues and silvers, which are frequently used in Palladium's architecture.

Haworth, one of the largest and most respected furniture manufacturers in the United States, asked Lorenc + Yoo Design to redesign its existing showroom spaces. The company wanted its spaces to complement product display and establish a bold identity expressing its vision, core values, and key "stories." The result is a visually dynamic environment that communicates on a variety of levels while solving pragmatic constraints.

A bold color palette of apple green and sky blue combined with black-and-white graphics, metaphorical images, and witty copy were employed to communicate Haworth's multifaceted nature. Color was applied in an architectonic manner, creating focal elements in the space, as well as dematerializing a forest of internal structural columns to form an artistic graphic composition.

To keep the experience fresh and interesting, the designers use color judiciously. Lorenc continues, "If one uses the entire color palette within all parts of the space, it doesn't work. It gets tiring. There needs to be a reason behind the use of color."

In environments, many spaces may be visible simultaneously, so the design can be seen in one overall glance. Thus the use of color becomes an organizing or thematic medium in Lorenc + Yoo Design's work. In addition, the designers look for equity their clients may have in a particular color scheme and incorporate that into the overall strategy. In exhibits, color is tied more directly to corporate identity and brand messaging, but it is used in a subtle way with punctuations of punchy color. For their work in signage, which tends to have greater longevity in terms of display usage, color and materials are tied to the interior design or the architecture of the building.

The firm has no set color palette, although the principals admit to using a lot of silver-colored metals, such as aluminum and stainless steel. Jan Lorenc describes color selections as "totally dependent on the intent of the project." He says, "We learn about the effects and intensities of colors to see what the space is like and build a digital or physical walk-through model. The physical model is the best way to see the space, since you can walk through it in your own mind at your own pace without the technology hindering your participation." Either way, the designers visualize the spatial sensation of their color choices before implementation.

Designed to stand in stark contrast to the visually hyperactive booths nearby, the Sony Ericsson Exhibit spells out the two capital letters of the newly formed company it represents. Simultaneously weighty and massive yet ethereal and fluid, the undulating planes of the *S* and *E* letterforms symbolize both the client's prominent positions of strength and its futuristic outlook. The two-level structure accommodates the dual nature of the exhibit.

Product demonstration and reception areas are on the first floor, and private conference space is on the second. Once inside the space, visitors occupy a surreal environment of technology, focused on previewing small electronic devices. The exhibit has a landmark quality and is a place within a place that boldly communicates the client's vision. Sony Ericsson

products speak to young adults. The exhibit's interior finishes and displays are intended to appeal to this market through style, color, and overall ambience. The color palette is simple and direct for bold visual impact. Though the display is predominantly white, accent colors echo the client's new identity.

# LUST
## The Hague, Netherlands

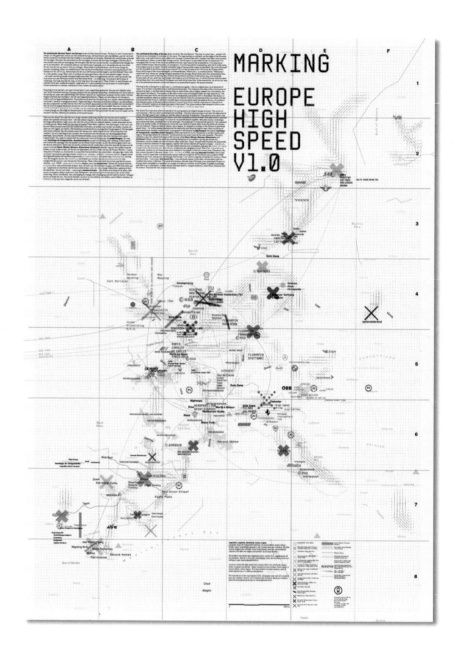

LUST is a design, typography, and propaganda collaborative based in The Hague that was started in 1996 by Thomas Castro and Jeroen Barendse. The studio accepts commissioned work—such as books, posters, websites, and interactive projects for architects, art groups, designers, and publishers—and also produces self-initiated work, including type design. LUST describes its work as "typography graphic design abstract cartography mapping random mistake-ism fonts type design multimedia interactive Web design internet www art abstract big bang chaos."

Underpinning its work is a point of view that becomes apparent when understanding how LUST defines the concept behind the name of its company. LUST is "coincidence and coincidentalism, the exaltation of the insignificant, the degradation of form and content to its essence, magnification, and contextuality versus textuality." The designers do concede, however, "No one interpretation of LUST is correct. Your conclusion is just as valid as ours. LUST is, after all, personal."

For LUST color is never a given or a must. It is another tool to use (or exploit) to communicate ideas. The designers use color to lend meaning to data visualization. Castro explains, "Because of our work methodology, there comes a point after the research phase where we are analyzing the data we have to design. At this stage, we use graphs, charts, tables, and matrices, so colors are used to define certain elements of the data to be able to understand them and how they fit with each other."

This map, made for Atelier HSL, is one of a series designed to spark passenger interest in traveling by Holland's high-speed train. This map addresses the idea that traveling is not only going from point A to B by crossing several intersections, highlighting interesting places the train passes that could be points of departure for passengers' adventures. The map presents travel stories in a short text written in both Dutch and English. Places mentioned in the text are tagged on the maps.

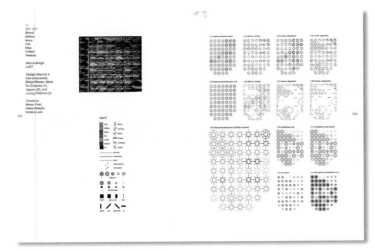

The copy invites the public to consider their own stories of the places and people they are visiting by train, thereby conceptually marking the map for themselves. A series of subdued yet highly transparent colors were used to represent the Xs and other markings to avoid cluttering the minute dots of the grid and flow lines of the rails. Silver was used for the grid and flow lines to add richness and depth.

*Margeting: Inventing a Different Marketing Language,* above, is a book that focuses on the consumer's participation in the process. A recurrent theme is the use of rhizome (or nonhierarchy) as a marketing approach. This structure is apparent in the book structure and page layouts. Two types of color are used: fluorescent navigational elements, and dark hues for italicized information.

Color is an extension of the designers' analytical methods and is aesthetically pleasing as well. Elements such as columns of text are colorful expressions of meaning and context. Colored grids add visual richness but also define a relative scale.

LUST's color palettes are always derived from what is being communicated and the medium used for communication. Castro says, "In our mapping work, it is important to have colors that are easily distinguished. Also, we tend to use colors that are based on 100-percent coverage of one or more of the CMYK colors." This choice is due to legibility and vibrancy of color. "For projects related to the screen," Castro continues, "colors are chosen for different reasons: saturation, color vibration, color temperature, glare, overscan, etc. These all relate." The designers have also experimented with randomly generated color, especially in their recent website work, but Thomas Castro states, "It is never an indiscriminate choice, even if the colors are generated randomly."

This series of three maps was designed to provide a self-guided tour of special projects built in the *Vinex* (government-developed communities of The Hague) for the celebration of the Day of Architecture in Holland. A colorful matrix navigation system designed as an index of projects by location and architect is the dominant visual identity. The designers chose not to use typical geographic color notations. The result is a fresh, contemporary take on mapping.

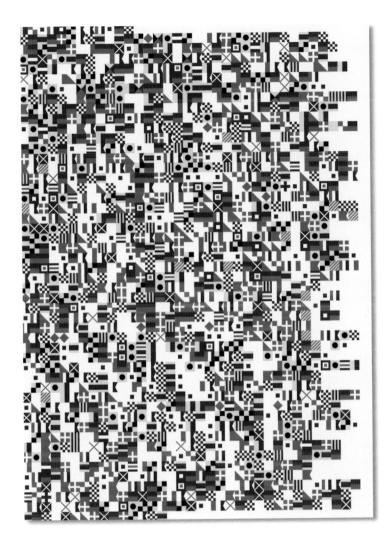

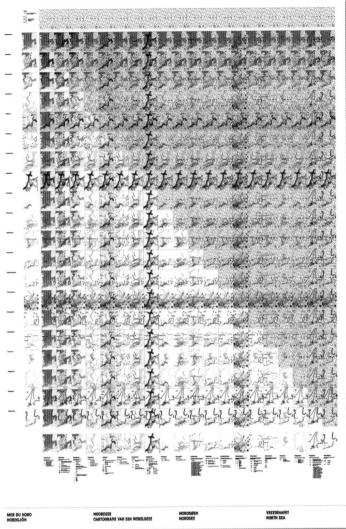

| MER DU NORD NORDSJÖN | NOORDZEE CARTOGRAFIE VAN EEN WERELDZEE | NORDSØEN NORDSEE | VESTERHAVET NORTH SEA |

LUST self-published this project, which stems from the research the designers did for a mapping project of Hoek van Holland (an area of Rotterdam bordering on the North Sea). There was much unused research, so the designers created *Noord Zee: Cartografie van eeen wereld zee* (*North Sea: Cartography of a World Sea*), an atlas of twenty topical maps that tie together historical, cultural, and geographical information in an interesting way. Essentially, this project investigates what could be called North Sea culture. The maps offer a range of information on the area's fishing, religions, ethnicity, shipwrecks, and more. Here again, transparent rich color adds to navigational ease, improved legibility, and visual texture. The content of the maps tends to be highly conceptual visual representations of information in which data become colorful graphic patterns.

# Methodologie, Inc.
## Seattle, USA

Methodologie is a brand firm that specializes in comprehensive, business-critical communications systems such as brand development, investor communications, corporate identity systems, and print and interaction design. The firm's work is mostly business to business, with a strong presence in the "yin" industries, such as technology, biotech, and property development, balanced by the "yang" of nonprofit, human services, and fine arts clients. The designers say, "The hard side and soft side of our client list influence each other for the better."

Methodologie is very much a collaborative team of twenty members, with five principals and two creative directors, probably best known for their annual report projects. However, the firm's branding and Web practices are full-fledged offerings that continue the tradition of blending great strategy with beautiful design in corporate communications.

Of color philosophy, Methodologie says, "Colors are very slippery. They are part science, part art, part intuition, part business. As soon as we try to make a pure science out of it—which some studies prove is possible—we find we over-think it." The designers' approach to color selection depends on the project, client, and context. "For an identity system where color plays a vital role and acts as a root system of the brand design, the colors need to be long lasting. In this case, we approach the selection of color deliberately and go through many rounds of color studies and revisions. We look at the client's competitive landscape to see how to stand out colorwise. The goal is really to own a color in a given category because it is unique but also because it so perfectly fits the brand," explains Methodologie.

Da Vinci Gourmet makes flavored syrups and sauces, typically used in espresso drinks by coffee house *baristas* the world over. Methodologie reinvented the company's identity and packaging to differentiate better among the items in the Da Vinci product line. The designers took a sophisticated, contemporary design approach by using translucent labels with solid white type that let the different syrups show through. Color appears only in the name of the flavor.

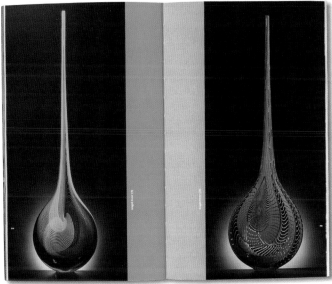

LINO
TAGLIAPIETRA
PASSIONE
*e vetro*
AT
WILLIAM
TRAVER GALLERY

BY WILLIAM TRAVER

I first met Lino Tagliapietra 25 years ago when he came to teach Venetian glassblowing techniques at Pilchuck Glass School. We had a small show for him at the gallery that summer, and the response to his work was overwhelming. From the beginning, I have been amazed by Lino's virtuosity; but over the years, my admiration for his talent has been surpassed by my respect for him as a person.

Much of what has been written about Lino throughout the years has focused on his technical skills and his standing in the international glass community. It is universally accepted that the Studio Glass Movement would not be the same without Lino Tagliapietra; yet I believe it is his spirit, his energy, his soul, and his passion that make his work truly outstanding.

Lino grew up steeped in the tradition of Venetian glass making. Even before becoming an apprentice in a glass factory at the age of eleven, he traveled through Muranese streets named for technical glassmaking terms and historical maestros. Throughout the course of his long and

The William Traver Gallery's catalog for an exhibition of Italian glass art master Lino Tagliapietra is a dramatic high-end piece. The design was driven by the artist's one-of-a-kind wonders of vibrant color and gravity-defying forms. The designers photographed the artworks in pristine isolation and then highlighted each piece with a band of color next to the photo. The rich color palette was sampled from the artwork photos so each color would complement or contrast the art perfectly. Methodologie chose a bright fuchsia cover and hot yellow and pink for the typography so there would be no question that the catalog and Lino's work are a passionate celebration of color.

For its annual report practice, Methodologie uses color in a flexible and fluid way because of the shorter lifespan of these projects. "There are two paths in the road of color for annual reports. If the annual is driven strictly by the corporate brand, then the color palette will most often be derived directly from the specific brand colors. The other option is for color to be driven by the story of the annual that year," explains Methodologie. "On the Web, it's a whole different story. Colors that work great in print don't always have the same effect digitally. And you have so little control over what the user's monitor settings are that, to some extent, you have to give yourself over to it."

Methodologie realizes that color palettes shift with the fashion tides and tries to "just keep that spinning wheel of color fortune in the back of our minds." The firm tends to think that it has no specific kind of color palette. Rather, Methodologie says, "We try to design for our clients, not ourselves. One of the roles of our creative director is to keep an eye on Methodologie trends, just to ensure that a color is being chosen because it is appropriate, not because it is top of mind and handy."

Safeco, a top U.S. insurance company, offers an annual agent incentive program, the prize being a luxury trip in which top agents can attend seminars and relax with their spouses and colleagues. The island of Kauai was the destination for this year's program. The brochure (above) shows off the romantic side of Hawaii with a dreamy watercolor palette of light sky blues and sea greens. The overlapping translucency of the stock heightens the watery effect.

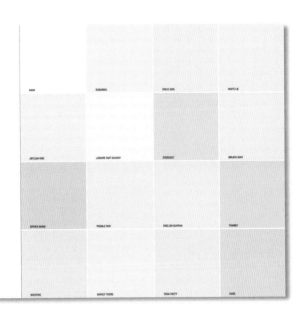

"**"I JUST WANT WHITE...**"

"Practically everybody leaves here with a can of white paint... But people are very picky about their choices. If there's too much hint of a green or a red or a blue, they'll just go nuts. It's really weird what kinds of people choose different whites. Who wants the palest kind of white? A single man wants that; a single man will rarely choose color. Artists, on the other hand, sometimes want a single clean white room, but the rest of their house will be rainbows."

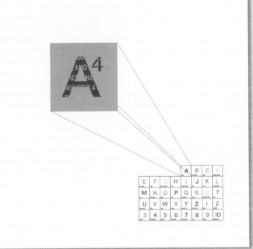

This is an image piece for the top West Coast commercial printer in the United States, Colorgraphics. The brochure, called "Speaking in Color," shows off the client's high-end printing capabilities and utilizes the theme of color. Methodologie developed the idea of asking people what color means to them.

The designers interviewed groups of people about the role that color plays in their lives and then used these rich stories and thoughts verbatim, bringing them to life. The quotes and stories drive the color system and illustrate the colors people talk about. However, the cover, introduction, and supporting text throughout the book are white and gray to be as neutral as possible in order to let the color stories take center stage.

# Morla Design
## San Francisco, USA

Morla Design has an eclectic body of work ranging from identity to environments to books. One element that unifies the work is an adventurous use of color. Creative director Jennifer Morla takes risks with color within the context of appropriateness for her clients and their target audiences. "Oftentimes they say that design is a seductive propaganda, but it's not always trying to pull the wool over somebody's eyes. Design has to excite, but it has to inform in a way that engages. I try to involve the audience in the design process, whether they know it or not." She succeeds in this goal, often aided by her use of color.

According to Morla, "Extremes work. Really large, or really thick, or really small, or really colorful, or really simple, or really dense." Morla's typical approach to color is to choose a palette of about five base colors that best represent the ideas being conveyed in the project. She then picks two lighter colors that might be transparent in order to overprint the base colors. To round out the palette, she selects two additional colors that are denser and perhaps darker than the base colors to use as contrast and provide the ability to reverse colors out of them. This approach has been an effective way to build color systems.

As Morla said in a recent keynote speech to designers, "Passion enables us to remain true to our creative vision. Analyze, synthesize, visualize, but don't compromise."

*This is a pair of Levi's jeans...* illustrates the past 140 years of Levi's 501 Jeans with more than 300 pages of people, places, and marketing that turned one brand into an American icon. The piece features eclectic typography, including vintage lettering, as well as western and historical imagery. The book has pull-out spreads that add to its visual interest. Additional

pages from the Levi's 501 jeans book show how Morla Design used color to recontextualize this iconic American brand for a contemporary audience. The designers did not use the obvious colors—blue for the denim or the browns and sepias of the original historic photographs. Instead the piece features archival imagery treated in a day-glo palette.

The choice of high-key colors is also reference to the San Francisco of the 1960s—when Levi's became a big brand. These images are posterized and translated into two colors, often using complementary pairs.

*Hemispheres* has won more awards than any other in-flight magazine in the United States, This piece was the first cover of the magazine after the September 11th tragedy, and Morla chose an upbeat color palette, using bright pastels. The design evokes a futuristic feeling that helped ease tensions and allowed passengers to relax and enjoy their flight.

DWR realized that though their residential business was thriving, they needed to strengthen their appeal to the design professional. *DWR Profile* addressed topical design and architecture issues while showcasing new product offerings. The DWR signature red is used throughout the publication to unify all branding efforts and ensure an understanding that this publication is connected to DWR stores and catalogs.

The Mexican Museum twentieth anniversary poster commemorates the museum's collection of pre-Columbian, colonial, and contemporary Mexican art. The large benday portrait of famed painter Frida Kahlo and the quintessential image of Our Lady of Guadalupe combined with Lotteria game card imagery and 19th-century Mexican wood-block type celebrate the varied heritage of Mexican arts and crafts.

For the U.S. bid city for the Summer 2012 Olympic Games, Morla chose not to create an overt interpretation of what 2012 might be but instead created a modern vision of the classic portrait poster—one that incorporates the optimism of the Olympic Games with a bold iconic image of an Asian-American swimmer. The radiating lines, energetic color palette, and posterized dot screens provide a modern take on the psychedelic posters of the 1960s that dominated the Haight-Ashbury counterculture and music graphics.

For the Discovery Channel, Morla Design created a total brand identity and packaging system for implementation throughout the company's retail stores. The project encompassed shopping bags, gift boxes, and product packaging. Surface graphics include geometric spiral illustrations that layer and move to create moiré patterns and reinforce the theme of discovery. Silk-screened, day-glo colors were used to attract young audiences, typically boys, and stand out in the stores' frenetic shopping mall locations.

Williams-Sonoma called upon Morla Design to create all consumer touch-points for its Hold Everything retail stores. The
catalog redesign is considerably lighter in appearance, with
the covers featuring a predominantly white image—chosen in
order to allow the product to be the star of the photo, to capture the inspirational aspects of these products by evoking
organization, and lastly, to permit the logo to stand out.

Kibu.com is an online company targeted to girls ages thir-
teen to eighteen. Morla Design identified brand objectives,
developed naming, created the identity, and designed every
consumer and trade touch-point. The palette is intentionally
trendy, spotlighting hot colors. High-key orange was chosen
as the basis for the dot identity so it would appeal to its young,
fashion-conscious audience.

# Collins
## New York / San Francisco, USA

At Collins, co-founder, Brian Collins and his team see a world where all points converge: digital into physical, consumer into producer, and biology into technology. They call it the Convergence Era. What was once siloed is now integrated and seamless. What were once passive experiences are now controlled by customers themselves. The consumer is the co-creator of the message.

Traditionally, a brand's success was tied to the product, service, and visual message. At Collins, they understand that today, success hinges not on only crafting a carefully controlled image, but on creating blended, unforgettable experiences that enrich people's lives. In today's business atmosphere, competitors can mimic products, slash prices, and outspend a media buy. But no competitor can replicate another brand's convergent brand experience.

They help leaders build remarkable brand experiences that are impossible to copy with a direct process: clarify their brand's authentic story, create new business value through design thinking, fix off-brand expressions, transform misaligned channels into one seamless experience, expand into new types of consumer engagement, and build platforms for consumer co-creation.

This is not simply an intellectual exercise. Collins uses color, imagery, and form to engage the audience, both internally and externally. The power of form is enhanced by the cohesive strategy across multiple media, while maintaining brand cohesion.

Vitaminwater has always had a strong design pedigree. When it launched in 2000 it took the market by storm with its minimal, colorful packaging and irreverent tone of voice. However, over the last 15 years an explosion of copycat products and a diluted identity led to a decline in market share and a repetitive brand expression.

Collins revitalized the brand through a new visual language. The solution was inspired by the original label and color of the product itself — a simple illustrated bottle paired with a diverse color palette and varied application. This system builds on their design heritage in a way that is authentic to the original brand yet crafted for a new audience. It also encourages far more flexibility in its expression while still keeping the product itself the focus.

GLACÉAU
**vitamin**water.

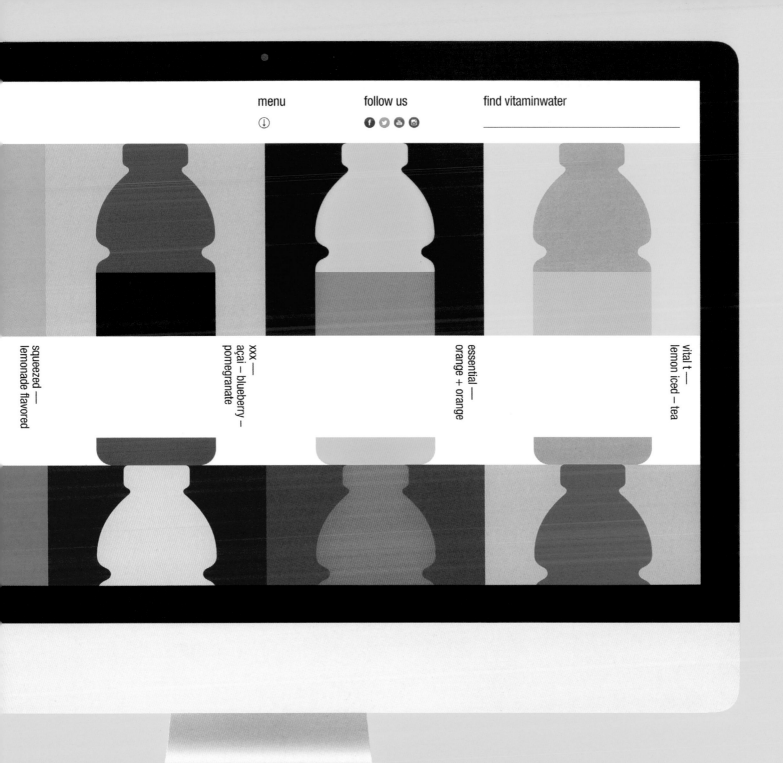

Collins worked closely with Ace Insurance during their acquisition of Chubb, defining the new company vision and helping build their new global brand. Collins designed a new visual system and identity for use on communications to digital services to its environments around the world. The color palette, saturated and sophisticated conveys a sense of optimism and freshness.

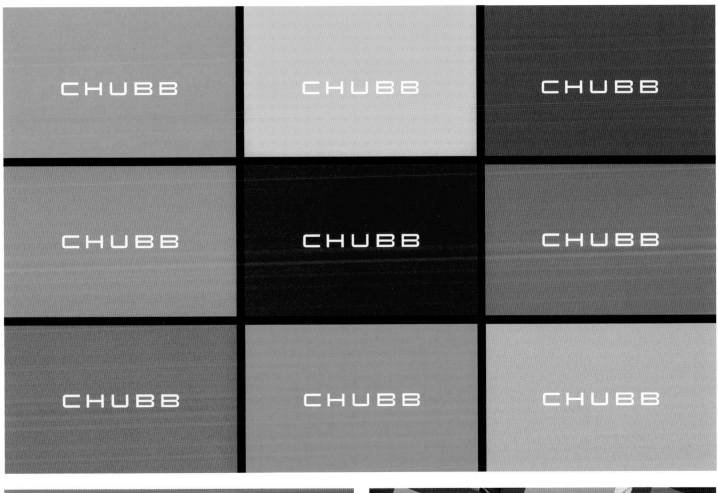

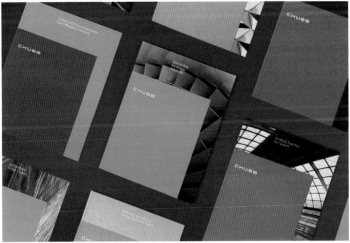

No category in skincare is easy to break into – but lip balm is particularly difficult. Undeterred, Eos asked Collins to work with them to launch the most beloved lip balm in the category. Women struggle to find lip balm in their cluttered purses. The reason is that almost all lip balm comes in a tube form, a generic form that, to the touch, can be mistaken for eye liner, lipstick, a pen, a roll of mints, etc. The strategy: Stand out by improving the packaging experience. In partnership with

Eos, we helped create packaging that could be recognized in the dark — or a cluttered bag – simply by touching it. We also defined an array of magnetic colors that cued flavor and caught the eye.Eos is now the number one selling lip balm. Teenagers change out the tops to signal they are dating. People take pictures of them, collect the flavors, knit holding cases for them, bedazzle them, and post videos about them on YouTube.

# Pentagram Design, Ltd.
## London, UK

Pentagram is one of the world's premiere design companies. The firm is notable for its work, its unique business structure, and its longevity. Not given to the styles and trends of the day, Pentagram's work stands the test of time, and the company has been thriving for thirty-three years.

Pentagram is a multinational, multidisciplinary collaboration of designers who do print and screen graphics, product and environmental design, and architecture. The firm is organized around its nineteen partners, all practicing designers, who work with small dedicated teams and share minimal corporate infrastructure and support personnel. Pentagram has offices in London, New York, San Francisco, Berlin, and Austin. The 138 staff members are augmented by a worldwide network of collaborators who contribute to the capabilities of the firm. "I suppose it is a bit of a cult," mused partner John McConnell in an article in FT.com (a division of London's *Financial Times*). "I suppose that's how we behave in some ways."

Since its 1972 London founding, Pentagram, named for its original five principals, has been one of the most influential graphic, product, and architectural firms in the world. The firm is known for its many partners' unique talents and idiosyncrasies. In addition, the firm has always allowed for and encouraged many voices in design, rather than adhere to strict orthodoxies about the way Pentagram work should look. Pentagram has an ideology

Pentagram was commissioned to create the name and brand identity for the Spanish confectioner company General de Confitería,. The name and design are suitable for global use, with a name pronounceable in any language and a palette of bright primary colors.

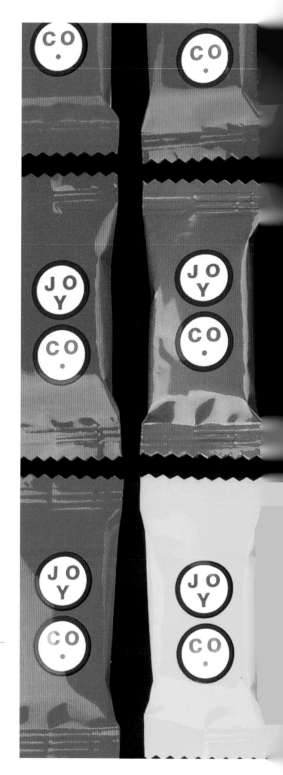

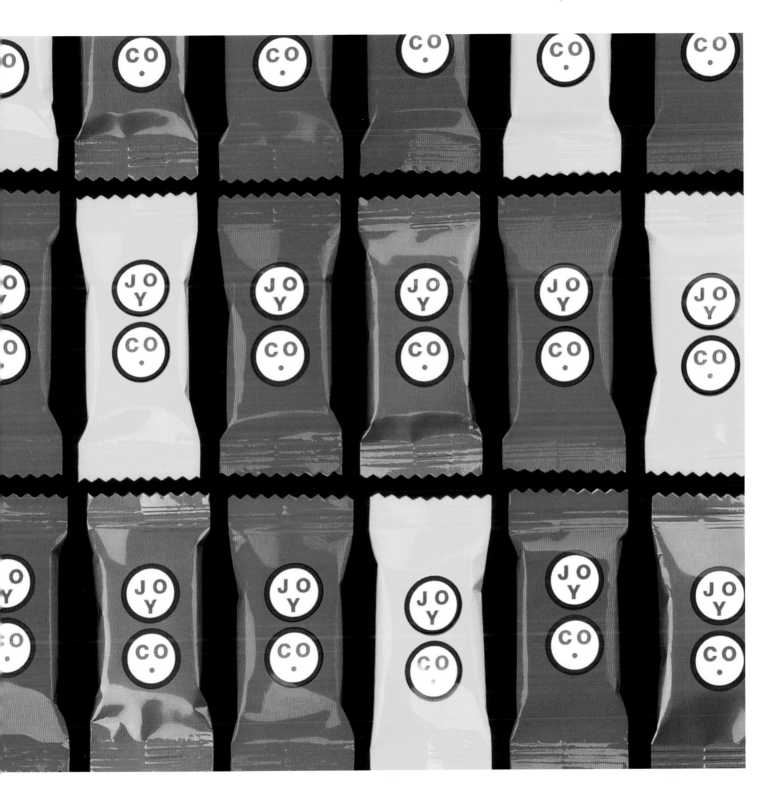

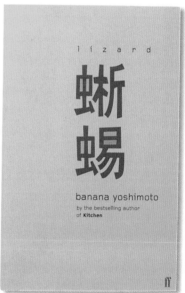

of idea-based design. This approach, says Randall Rothenberg in *Pentagram Book Five*, "asserted that design communicated both viscerally and intellectually, that it gratified the soul at the same time it satisfied the mind.

As such, communication through design could not be achieved by the imposition of a strict set of rules or by the intrusion of an artistic vision." Each problem is unique and therefore invites a single solution appropriate to the problem—and that is essentially the designers' color philosophy as well. Color choices are made intelligently in keeping with the demands of each project.

Featured here are projects from Pentagram's European offices, representing the work of some of the eight partners and fifty employees, including principals David Hillman, John McConnell, Justus Oehler, and John Rushworth, along with designers Mathew Richardson, Jan Pluer, Liza Enebeis, Rob Duncan, and Hazel Macmillan. These pieces illustrate the variety of ways in which Pentagram's idea-based approach plays out in terms of color.

Over the last twenty years, Pentagram has worked extensively for U.K. publisher Faber & Faber. Recent redesigns employ vibrant colors and strong typography. For the reprint of a series of Banana Yoshimoto's fiction, Pentagram designed a visual language that unifies the body of work while suggesting the individual qualities of each book.

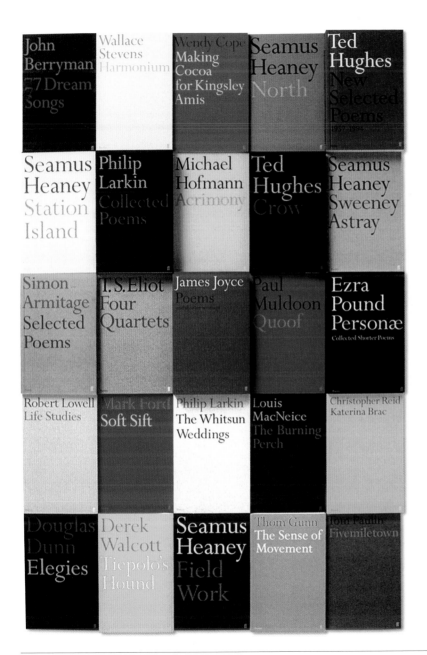

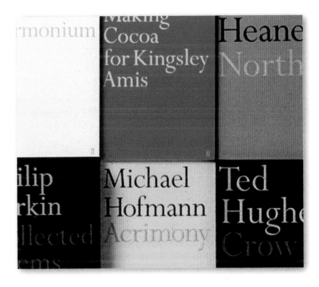

The Faber poetry series is also devoid of imagery, again using color to express the central mood and emotional content of each book. The covers of the poetry series each use a limited palette of three colors: one for the author's name, one for the title, and one for the background. Yoshimoto's covers feature strong, Japanese character–based typography, while the poetry covers utilize Perpetua, a distinctive classical font.

# The Waterways Trust
*Everyone valued, everyone involved*

Review 2001/2002

Pentagram's design for The Waterways Trust features black-and-white photography over-laid by a rich aquatic blue. The effect is rather somber, but the blue seems to symbolize the possibility that the stark landscape can be brought back to life.

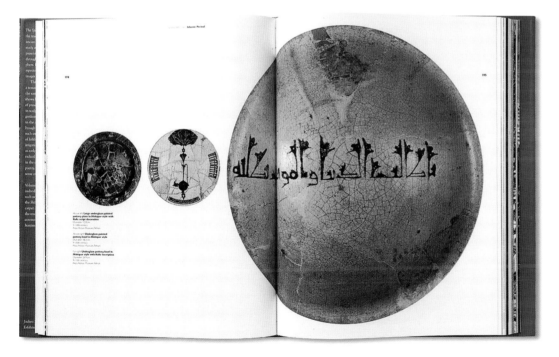

*The Splendor of Iran* provides unprecedented insight into the traditions and contemporary life of one of the world's most enduring civilizations. The first comprehensive study of Persian culture since the 1930s, it is the result of a unique five-year collaboration combining Iranian scholarship, insight, and photographic access with international design and publishing.

Most of the books' color comes from the series of specially commissioned photographs. These depict ancient traditions that still affect the life and customs of present-day Iran in almost every sphere of human activity, including the decorative arts, science and medicine, philosophy, and poetry.

# Segura, Inc.
## Chicago, USA

Born in Cuba and a refugee from the Cuban Revolution, Segura immigrated to Miami in the 1960s. He started as a musician who developed flyers for his band and later evolved into a self-taught designer/art director for ad agencies before moving to Chicago. There he founded Segura, Inc., in 1991. He and his partner/wife, Sun, head an international group of designers who produce graphic design, print advertising, logos, catalogs, annual reports, corporate identities, posters, and new media for carefully chosen clients. Segura says, "Whatever the medium, we create marketing messages people notice and respond to, with a distinctive sense of style and simplicity that stands the test of time."

In an interview for a Taiwanese magazine, writer Jimmy Cuen asked Carlos Segura what was special about his studio. Segura replied, "We are very conscious of the client. We always deliver executions based on a relevant concept and not an out-of-context style .... We put the 'strategical' needs of a client ahead of our stylistic needs or desires, and we always target the intended market, even at the expense of the client's personal wishes. This approach of putting client needs first means that the firm has no set color philosophy. Color is chosen based on "whatever color we feel is appropriate for the task. We do not follow a rule for this, since it greatly depends on the body language of the project," explains Segura.

However, Segura does admit to the desire to blend and explore the fine art side of the business of design, not just the commercial. This edge remains visible in all of the studios' work.

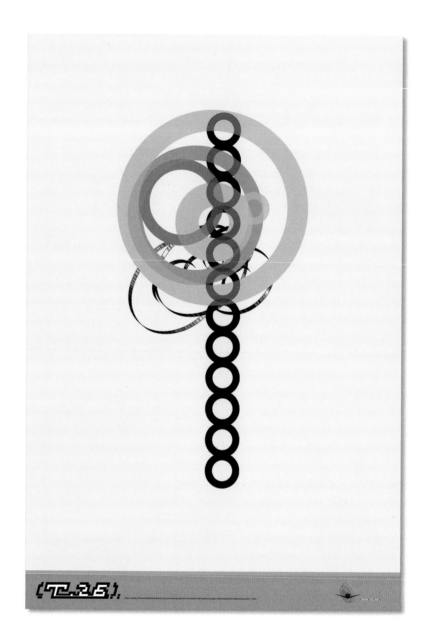

Segura's [T-26] digital type foundry was founded in 1994 in the middle of the postmodern typographic experimentation era. The company has become one of the best-known and globally influential modern type design foundries. [T-26] has stayed current, evolving from the grunge and hip-hop fonts that made it an instant hit with a new generation of computer-literate designers.

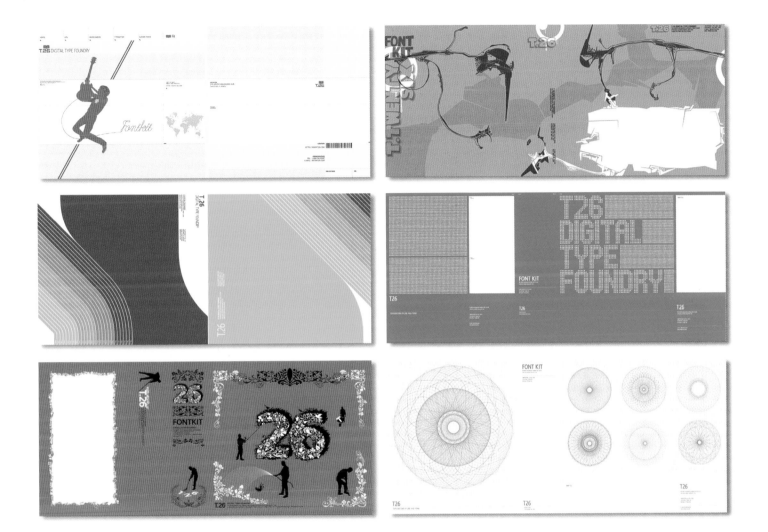

Segura, Inc., continually does interesting and innovative work on behalf of its subsidiary, [T-26]. Because the [T-26] fonts tend to break the traditional boundaries and notions of letterforms, so do its promotions. The poster shows what might be called a classical approach with a modern edge, utilizing a subtle, nearly neutral color palette. The variety of [T-26] packs are a riot of graphic styles and color schemes.

[T-26] includes more than 600 typefaces designed by 250-plus type designers from around the world. The packs therefore must convey the breadth of the product offering as well as provide demonstrations of effective font use. Segura sees the [T-26] packages as more "gift" than "sales pitch," so the pieces tend to resemble limited-edition artworks. The [T-26] kits are produced using a variety of techniques including letterpress, silkscreen, offset, and woodblock prints.

hold edges

**T-26 DIGITAL TYPE FOUNDRY**
1110 NORTH MILWAUKEE AVENUE, FIRST FLOOR
CHICAGO, ILLINOIS 60622,4017 USA.  1.888.T26.FON
TELEPHONE  773. 862. 1201.  FACSIMILE  773. 862. 12
E-MAIL  INFO@T26.COM.  WEB  WWW.T26.COM

**T-26 DIGITAL TYPE FOUNDRY**
1110 NORTH MILWAUKEE AVENUE, FIRST FLOOR
CHICAGO, ILLINOIS 60622.4017 USA, 1.888.T26.FONT (US.TOLL.FREE)
TELEPHONE 773. 862. 1201. FACSIMILE 773. 862. 1214
E-MAIL INFO@T26.COM. WEB WWW.T26.COM

# Steinbranding
## Buenos Aires, Argentina

Steinbranding consists of more than sixty professionals and fifty designers committed to inspiring and revitalizing brands. Clients are primarily entertainment companies based in Latin America, but Steinbranding does have a variety of corporate clients and has branded two airports, one in Argentina and one in Armenia. Steinbranding calls their work "design for the southern hemisphere."

Primarily known for branding television networks and developing on-air promotions and show packages, the firm also creates off-air graphics in both print and Web formats. With more than fifteen years of experience in branding Hispanic television markets, Steinbranding has often handled the Latin American presence of U.S. television networks. Creative director Guillermo Stein says, "An unprecedented visual language characterizes our present and immediate future. The language is 'glocal'— where the global and the local blend. It is where all cultures connect without losing their identity." Stein continues, "'Glocal' design revolutionized the local market by connecting it to the world while keeping global languages from becoming empty and predictable."

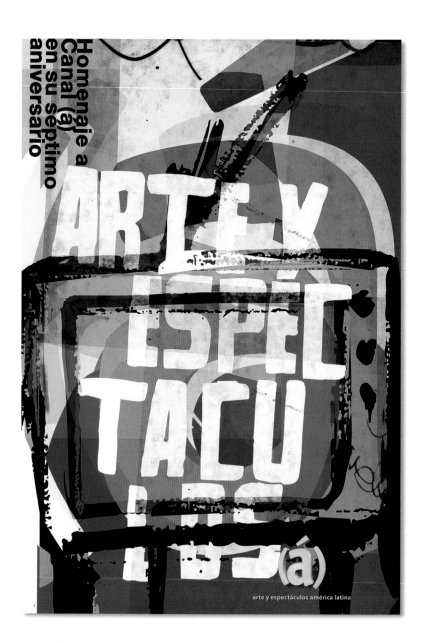

A large part of Steinbranding's work is to create the off-air promotions that coordinate with and support their on-air network identity packages. This is a poster for Colombia's Canal (á) television network. The lively graphics and bright colors are meant to appeal to Spanish-speaking audiences. Overlapping color blocks and rough typography give the poster a hand-hewn authenticity.

A slightly retro graphic style coupled with a muted palette work together to represent the alchemy and seduction of food—its scents, flavors, and colors. There is a Pop Art quality to this promotional poster's design that honors the pleasures of food as the symbolic center of a certain lifestyle. The art of good living is positioned as a virtue to the audience.

For Cosmopolitan Televisión, a Spanish-language television network based on the famous women's magazine, the visual language is about modern femininity. The promotional poster plays with a different set of iconography representing contemporary women. A palette of muted colors provides a backdrop to a dressmaker's dummy, creating depth and dimension while working as both a metaphor and a decorative device.

Steinbranding is culturally sensitive and seeks to respect the differences that make each Spanish-speaking country distinct not only from one another but from the United States. The designers look to strike a new balance between cultures because, as they observe, "*Hispanic* is not the same as *Latino*. The challenge is how to capture these differences."

Steinbranding develops experiences for international audiences. Its images come alive on-air and off-air in breathtaking visual solutions rich with color. Its work is simultaneously poetic and gritty, rough yet grand. The firm works to create "design that illuminates the depths, [exposing] what lies beneath the surface." Color often becomes a powerful ally in conveying what is most essential about the client's message. Bright high-key palettes instantly attract attention, while dark restless areas pull the viewer to deeper awareness. The designers often set real-world colors aside and experiment with new ideas as they seek to develop design that involves more than one read—a literal one and a metaphorical one—that conveys a message. Steinbranding is an experimental laboratory for design, always seeking a new method of communicating with increasingly global audiences.

In this promo for El Gourmet's *Asador Urbano* (*Urban Grillmaster*), Steinbranding features the show's host together with graphic elements in the lime green of the network's identity. Lime green is used throughout all on-air and off-air graphics for El Gourmet as a unifying device.

For El Gourmet, Steinbranding created programming and daily on-air promos, end pages and spots, as well as off-air graphics such as invitations, posters, and a website. The network and its companion online presence focus on food, celebrating its role in daily life and society. Steinbranding developed a cheerful, colorful, spontaneous design system with a sense of humor. In this network ID, El Gourmet on-air talent is featured in clean white uniforms against stark white backgrounds. Simple type and repeating patterns of food and beverage elements play behind the figures. The El Gourmet logo appears frequently to provide cohesive branding.

The Europa Europa Television Network's tagline is "Return to The Old World: Revalorization of Authentic Cinema." Steinbranding used this point of view as inspiration for this handmade, attention-grabbing orange poster, which promotes the channel in a fresh way.

Film & Arts Network is a channel that seeks to reposition film as an art form. The challenge is to communicate and represent film as an artistic language and active movement rather than focus on the commercial aspects of movies. The graphics for the show *Big Bangs* are stark black and white and take form as musical notations that mutate, multiply, move away, and then reappear. The poster created to promote the network features the abstract play of transparent surfaces and typographic elements. A subdued palette of primary colors and grays subtly enhances the transparency effect of the floating planes of information. Both projects are sophisticated modern design solutions.

# Volume Inc.
## San Francisco, California

Founded by Adam Brodsley and Eric Heiman, Volume Inc. is one of the leading design firm's in California. The work ranges from identity, environmental, exhibitions, screen based media, to print. Their approach challenges preconcieved concepts of "polite" design. Within this context, they work with multiple attitudes, from punk rocker or neo-soul crooner. In addition to the formal excellence of the work, the solutions are smart, unexpected, and emotionally powerful.

At Volume, they still like to make beautiful things because, as they make clear, "beauty still counts." That, however, doesn't reduce the work to only pretty. They like to ask questions, at some points, perhaps, too many, but this inquisitive approach leads to a smoother process and better results. This helps clarify the right audience, which is one of Volume's greatest talents; to surgically communicate to the exact right group of viewers.

There is no one color philosophy, Volume's work is big and small, funny and sad, commercial and cultural, on screen and in your hands, and its bright orange and slate gray. They pride themselves on never doing the same thing twice.

In their own words, "We kick it with the how. Yes, the how. How we look at the world and solve problems. How we evaluate what you do and don't need. How we engage audiences and get them excited. How we find the best people to collaborate with and produce the best results. How-dy! We're Volume. Pleased to meet you."

For Pivot, the 2011 AIGA National Conference identity and collateral Volume included the identity guidelines that speak to the conceptual underpinnings. The color palette was inspired in its variety by the Pivot conference theme and is an extension of the dynamic identity they designed. The colors were inspired by the vitality of Phoenix culture and the natural landscape.

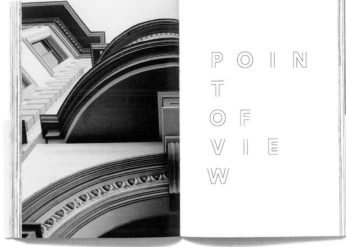

Volume always saw the See For Yourself book as a combination of how-to manual and meditative journal. The orange cover acts as a beacon—SEE this!—almost like a road construction cone. But the book is about teaching how to see the subtle visual patterns in the everyday world and so the cover wraps and interior color recedes to highlight the variety of the photography. The selective use of the beige background color in the interior complement the special sections that read more like journal-entries.

Volume created an environment for the Robert Wood Johnson Foundation "Building a Culture of Health" TED conference. On a practical level this environment provided a refuge from the conference where people could get coffee and watch the live TED telecast. On a brand level, Volume engaged people by asking them the question, "what does a culture of health mean to you?" and writing their answers on the blocks for everyone to see and enable further participation. The blue and green are RWJF brand colors, but Volume added another "color" with the wood (no pun intended!) material and texture that brings a more tactile, imperfect quality that echoes the human-centered goal of the health initiative.

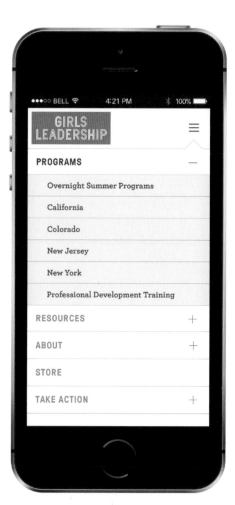

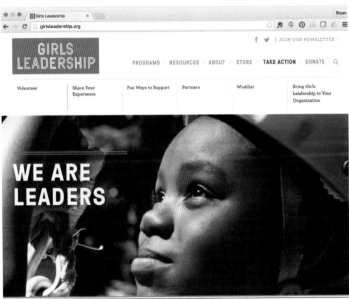

For the Girls Leadership brand identity and website, Volume included the brand guidelines that outline the inspiration. The identity speaks to the organization's desire to amplify the strength, emotional depth, and complexity of girls. The logo speaks simultaneously to strength and complexity. The colors were specifically chosen to reinforce these attributes and speak to the strength (red) and the emotional depth (plum).

# Gallery: Identity

1

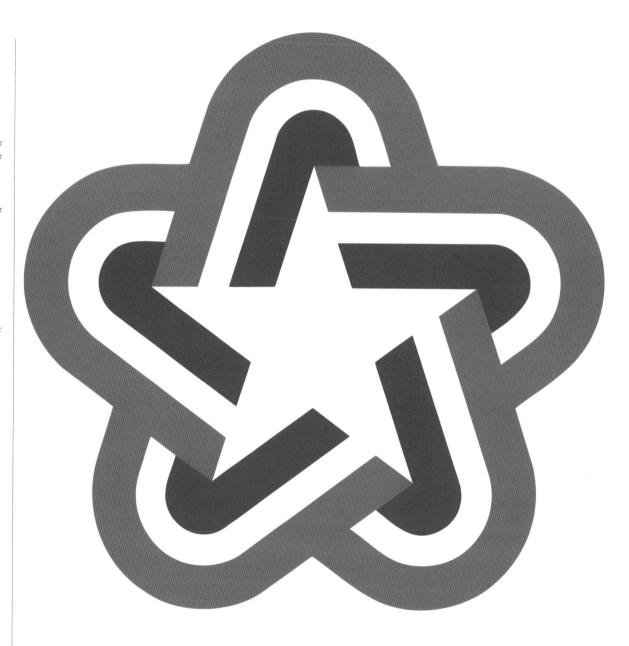

2

3 for the dogs

4 ®

5 filmforum

6 SHOWTIME

7 selecti on

8

9 PARCO NAZIONALE DEL VESUVIO

10 UBS Network

11 ATRIUM restavracija à la carte

12

13 M 2006 SALZBURG ART

14

15 NBC

16 FISH PACK®

17 Milk

18 M

19 POLNA SKLEDA restavracija

20 (BUR) NIN-GSET (TLE) RSC-ABIN

21 LIVE living in modern environments

22 redley

23 A

24

25

# Gallery: Web

 344 Design

 Sean Adams

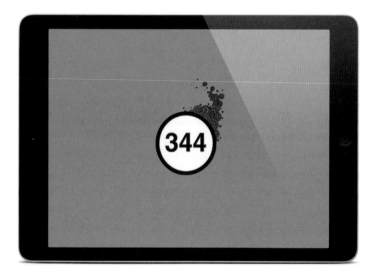

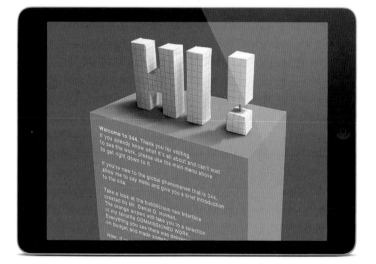

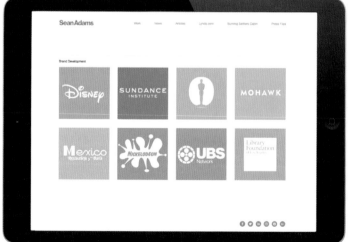

 Hello Design

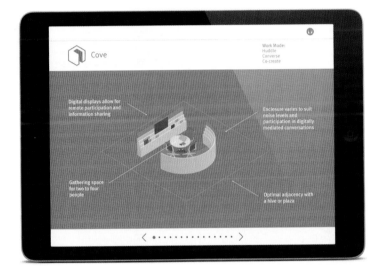

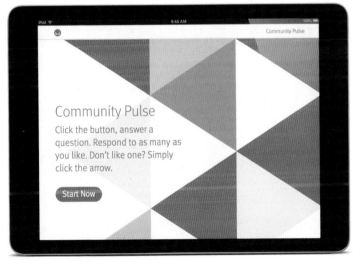

# Gallery: Corporate Communications

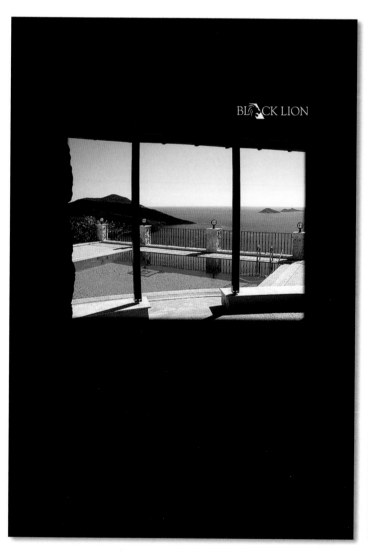

 Chimera Design

 C375

 Pentagram

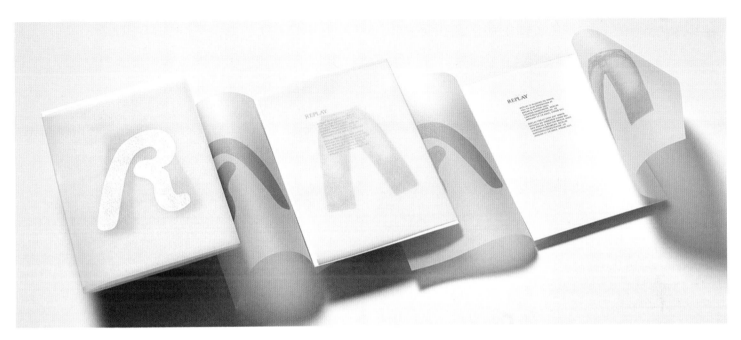

 Usine Des Boutons

 KROG

# Gallery: Posters

 Collins

 Collins

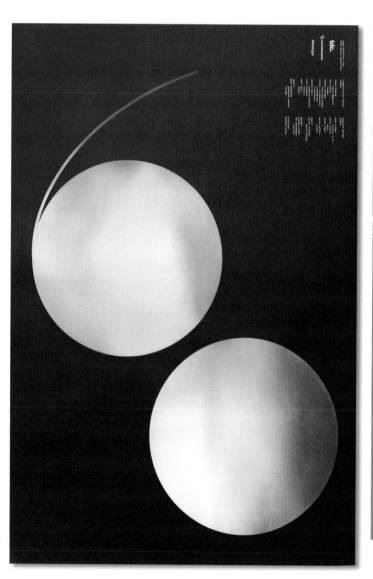

Sean Adams

Friend of a
Friend

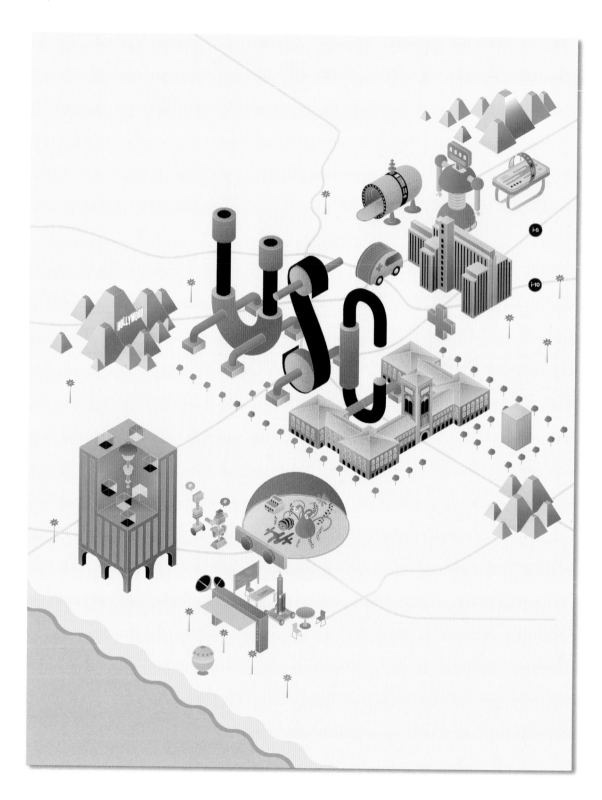

 blue river design

# CHEAP DATE

**Free admission to all exhibitions at BALTIC.**

5 galleries, 2 restaurants, café bar and shop. Open 7 days a week.
Click on www.balticmill.com to plan your visit.

BALTIC is a 15 minute walk from Newcastle Central Station
via Gateshead Millennium Bridge.

**BALTIC** BALTIC Centre for Contemporary Art,
Gateshead Quays, UK
Tel +44 (0)191 478 1810 www.balticmill.com

# GET RICH QUICK

**Discover a wealth of art for free at BALTIC.**

5 galleries, 2 restaurants, café bar and shop. Open 7 days a week.
Click on www.balticmill.com to plan your visit.

BALTIC is a 15 minute walk from Newcastle Central Station
via Gateshead Millennium Bridge.

**BALTIC** BALTIC Centre for Contemporary Art,
Gateshead Quays, UK
Tel +44 (0)191 478 1810 www.balticmill.com

# Glossary

**Achromatic** is the state of possessing no discernible hue and being without color.

**Additive colors** are produced by superimposing red, green, and blue light rays. All of these colors combine to create white light. Computer monitors and television screens use additive color.

**Advancing colors** appear nearer to the observer than receding colors. Warmer, higher-chroma, and lighter-valued colors tend to advance.

**Afterimages** are complementary color images generated by the eye in response to over-stimulation or retinal fatigue.

**Analogous colors** are hues that are adjacent on the color wheel.

**Blends** are areas of an image that transition from one color to another. Blends are also called *graduated tints* or *graduations*.

**Brilliance** is the quality of high light reflection and strong hue typically found in saturated colors.

**Brightness** is the amount of light reflected by a particular color. Brightness is also called *value*.

**Chroma** is the relative purity or strength of a hue, or its freedom from white, black, and gray. Chroma is a synonym for *intensity* and *saturation*.

**CIE** stands for Commission International de l'Eclairage, an international color consortium.

**CMYK** stands for cyan, magenta, yellow, and black, the colors of the subtractive color system used in offset lithography printing. They are also called *process colors*.

**Color** is a perceptual sensation created in the human mind in response to certain wavelengths of electromagnetic energy that constitute the visible spectrum of light. Human perception of and response to these wavelengths is affected by many factors including physiology, psychology, language, and culture.

**Colorimetry** is the technical term for the scientific measurement of color.

**Color constancy** is the ability of the human eye and brain to perceive colors accurately under a variety of lighting conditions, compensating automatically for any differences.

**Color correction** is the process of adjusting the color values of an image to correct or compensate for errors in photography, scanning, or separation.

**Color reduction** is the process of reducing the number of colors in a digital image in order to make the file smaller.

**Color schemes** are harmonious color combinations that use any two or more colors. The six classic color schemes are *monochromatic, analogous, complementary, split complementary, triadic,* and *tetradic* (also called *double complementary*).

**Color separation** is the process of separating images and artwork into cyan, magenta, yellow, and black in preparation for printing.

**Color space** is the range of colors achievable by any single reproduction device.

**Color tetrads** are sets of four colors, equally spaced on the color wheel, that contain a primary color, its complement, and a complementary pair of intermediaries. The term can also indicate any organization of color on the wheel forming a rectangle that could include a double split complement.

**Color triads** are sets of three colors, equally spaced on the color wheel, that form an equilateral triangle.

**Color wheels** are circular diagrams representing the spectrum of visible colors and illustrating their relationships.

**Complementary colors** are two colors opposite each other on the color wheel. They tend to intensify each other when used together and create a neutral color when mixed.

**Cool colors** are greens, blues, and violets.

**Duotones** are two-color halftones reproduced from a black-and-white or color photograph. The term can also mean a halftone image rendered in two colors.

**Fugitives** are ink colors that easily fade or deteriorate.

**Gamut** is the range of colors available within a certain color space.

**Ground** is the area that surrounds the central element or figure in a composition. Another term is *background*.

**Harmony** is a pleasing subjective state that occurs when two or more colors are used in combination.

**Hue** is the attribute of a color, defined by its dominant wavelength and position in the visible spectrum, that distinguishes it from other colors. The term can also indicate the name of a color.

**Intensity** is a synonym for *chroma*, which is the relative purity or strength of a hue.

**Intermediate colors**, also called *tertiary colors*, are made by mixing a secondary and a primary color together.

**Lightness** is the blackness or whiteness of a color.

**Luminance** is the brightness of a color.

**Metamerism** is the undesirable phenomenon that occurs when two colors that appear to match under one set of light conditions do not match under another set of conditions.

**Monochromatic** is the state of containing only one color.

**Neutral colors** are black, gray, white, browns, beiges, and tans. They do not appear on color wheels.

**Optical color mixing**, also called *partitive color*, is a perception of color that results from the combining of adjacent color by the eye and brain.

**Palette** is a group of colors used by a designer in a specific design.

**PANTONE Matching System (PMS)** is a patented system of inks, color specifications, and color guides used for reproducing colors.

**Primary colors** are pure hues from which all other colors can be mixed. They cannot be made by combining other hues. The artist's mixing primaries are red, yellow, blue (RYB); the additive primaries are red, green, blue (RGB); and the subtractive primaries are cyan, magenta, yellow (CMY).

**Process color** is four-color reproduction that uses four printing plates, one for each of the subtractive primary colors: cyan (process blue), magenta (process red), yellow (process yellow), plus black (process black).

**Profile** is the colorimetric description of the behavior of an input or output device that can be used by a computer application to ensure accurate transfer of color data. A profile describing the color space used during the image creation or editing should ideally be embedded in the image so it can later serve as a reference for other users, software applications, or display and output devices.

**RGB** stands for red, green, and blue, the primary colors of the additive color model.

**RYB** stands for red, yellow, and blue, the artist's primary colors, which are the basis of much color theory taught in art and design schools.

**Saturation** is the measure of the purity of a hue as determined by the amount of gray it contains. The higher the gray level is, the lower the saturation. Saturation is a synonym of *chroma*.

**Secondary colors** are made by mixing two primary colors.

**Shades** are hues mixed with black to form another darker color.

**Simultaneous contrast** is a human perception anomaly in which colors are affected by adjacent colors.

**Spot color** is a single solid or screened color printed using one printing plate, as opposed to a process color printed using two or more plates.

**Subtractive colors** are those produced by reflected light. Cyan, magenta, and yellow inks printed on white paper absorb, or subtract, the red, green, and blue portions of the spectrum. Subtractive color mixing is the basis of printed color.

**Tertiary colors** are formed by combining two secondary colors or by combining a primary with an adjacent.

**Tints** are hues mixed with white to form another lighter color. The term also refers to a solid color screened to less that 100 percent to create a lighter shade.

**Tones** are created by mixing a pure hue with its complement or gray.

**Triadic schemes** are color schemes using three colors that are spaced evenly around the color wheel.

**Value** is the relative lightness or darkness of a color. High value is light; low value is dark.

**Vanishing boundaries** occur when two different solid color areas of exactly the same value are placed next to each other; the hard edge separating the two colors seems to soften or disappear.

**Vibrating boundaries** occur when two different solid color areas, usually near complements of near equal value, are placed next to each other; the result is a noticeable optical fluttering effect.

**Visible spectrum** is the full range of visible hues. The rainbow is a naturally occurring manifestation of the visible spectrum.

**Warm colors** are reds, oranges, and yellows.

# Index

# Bibliography

# Web Resources

Albers, Josef. *Interaction of Color.* New Haven, CT: Yale University Press, 1963.

Carter, Rob. *Digital Color and Type.* Mies, Switzerland: RotoVision, 2002.

Fraser, Tom, and Adam Banks. *Designer's Color Manual: The Complete Guide to Theory and Application.* San Francisco: Chronicle, 2004.

Hollis, Richard. *Concise History of Graphic Design.* London: Thames & Hudson, 2001.

Itten, Johanes. *Itten: The Elements of Color.* New York: Van Nostrand Reinhold, 1970.

Kobayashi, Shigendbu. *Colorist: A Practical Handbook for Personal and Professional Use.* Tokyo: Kodansha, 1998.

Meggs, Philip B. *Type & Image: The Language of Graphic Design.* New York: Van Nostrand Reinhold, 1992.

Ocvirk, Otto G., Robert E. Stinson, Philip K. Wigg, Robert O. Bone, and David Cayton. *Art Fundamentals: Theory and Practice, 8th Edition.* New York: McGraw-Hill, 1998.

Poynor, Rick. *Obey the Giant.* London: August Media, 2001.

Sutherland, Rick, and Barb Karg. *Graphic Design Color Handbook: Choosing and Using Color from Concept to Final Output.* Beverly, MA: Rockport, 2003.

Sutton, Tina, and Bride M. Whelan. *The Complete Color Harmony.* Beverly, MA: Rockport, 2004.

Walch, Margaret, and Augustine Hope. *Living Colors: The Definitive Guide to Color Palettes Through the Ages.* San Francisco: Chronicle, 1995.

Wong, Wucius. *Principles of Color Design: Designing with Electronic Color.* New York: Van Nostrand Reinhold, 1997.

Additional useful color information can be obtained from the following websites.

www.adobe.com
www.albersfoundation.org
www.bartleby.com
www.color.org
www.colormarketing.org
www.colormatters.com
www.findarticles.com
www.pantone.com
www.wikipedia.org
www.wordiq.com

## About the Author

Sean Adams is the Executive Director of the Graphic Design
Graduate Program at ArtCenter, founder of Burning Settlers
Cabin studio, and on-screen author for lynda.com/Linked In.
He is the only two term AIGA national president in AIGA's 100
year history. In 2014, Adams was awarded the AIGA Medal, the
highest honor in the profession.

He is an AIGA Fellow, and Aspen Design Fellow. He has been
recognized by every major competition and publication including; *How, Print, Step, Communication Arts, Graphis*, AIGA, The
Type Directors Club, The British Art Director's Club, and the
Art Director's Club. Adams has been exhibited often, including
a solo exhibition at The San Francisco Museum of Modern Art.
Adams is the author of multiple magazine columns, and several best-selling books.

He has been cited as one of the forty most important people
shaping design internationally, and one of the top ten influen-
tial designers in the United States. Previously, Adams was a
founding partner at AdamsMorioka. His clients have included
Abrams, The Academy of Motion Picture Arts and Sciences,
Disney, Mohawk Fine Papers, The Metropolitan Opera,
Richard Meier & Partners, Sundance, and the University of
Southern California.